VOLUME FIVE
Japanese Navy Zero Fighters
(land-based)
New Guinea and the Solomons 1942-1944

MICHAEL JOHN CLARINGBOULD
WITH ED DEKIEP & RYAN TOEWS

Avonmore Books

Pacific Profiles Volume Five

Japanese Navy Zero Fighters (land-based)
New Guinea and the Solomons 1942-1944

Michael John Claringbould

ISBN: 978-0-6489262-4-5

First published 2021 by Avonmore Books

Avonmore Books
PO Box 217
Kent Town
South Australia 5071
Australia

Phone: (61 8) 8431 9780
avonmorebooks.com.au

A catalogue record for this
book is available from the
National Library of Australia

Cover design & layout by Diane Bricknell

Cover artwork captions

(Front cover) These four Zeros epitomise the diversity of colours in the Pacific theatre from 1942 to 1944. They are (top to bottom):

- *the personal Model 22 of No. 582 Ku chutaicho, Lieutenant Commander Shindo Saburo, the double yellow chevrons indicating his chutaicho status;*
- *Model 21 U-167 one of three participants in No. 6 Ku's first patrol from Buka on 8 October 1942, flown that day by shotaicho FPO1c Okazaki Seiki;*
- *Tainan Ku Model 21 V-117 flown by buntaicho Lieutenant Yamashita Joji, shot down at Milne Bay on 27 August 1942;*
- *No. 251 Ku Model 22 tail code 53-157 which operated from Lakunai throughout August 1943.*

(Back Cover) Warrant Officer Hidaka Hatsuo, a No. 204 Ku shotaicho, takes on a 339th FS Lightning over Bougainville in mid-1943. Hidaka took a detachment of No. 204 Ku Zeros to Buin at the beginning of February 1943 and for the first half of the year often accompanied his hikotaicho Miyano Zenjiro on missions.

Contents

The author at the site of the former Japanese Vunakanau airfield, near Rabaul, in 2006.

About the Author

Michael Claringbould – Author & Illustrator

Michael spent his formative years in Papua New Guinea in the 1960s, during which he became fascinated by the many WWII aircraft wrecks which still lie around the country. Michael has served widely overseas as an Australian diplomat, including in South East Asia and throughout the South Pacific where he had the fortune to return to Papua New Guinea for three years commencing in 2003.

Michael has authored and illustrated various books on Pacific War aviation. His history of the Tainan Naval Air Group in New Guinea, *Eagles of the Southern Sky*, received worldwide acclaim as the first English-language history of a Japanese fighter unit, and was translated into Japanese. An executive member of Pacific Air War History Associates, Michael holds a pilot license and PG4 paraglider rating. He continues to develop his skills as a digital 3D aviation artist, using 3DS MAX, Vray and Photoshop to attain markings accuracy.

Other Books by the Author

Black Sunday (2000)

Eagles of the Southern Sky (with Luca Ruffato, 2012)

Nemoto's Travels - The illustrated saga of a Japanese floatplane pilot in the first year of the Pacific War (Avonmore Books, 2021)

Operation I-Go Yamamoto's Last Offensive – New Guinea and the Solomons April 1943 (Avonmore Books, 2020)

P-39 / P-400 Airacobra versus A6M2/3 Zero-sen New Guinea 1942 (Osprey, 2018)

P-47D Thunderbolt versus Ki-43 Hayabusa New Guinea 1943/44 (Osprey, 2020)

Pacific Adversaries Volume One: Japanese Army Air Force vs The Allies New Guinea 1942-1944 (Avonmore Books, 2019)

Pacific Adversaries Volume Two: Imperial Japanese Navy vs The Allies New Guinea & the Solomons 1942-1944 (Avonmore Books, 2020)

Pacific Adversaries Volume Three: Imperial Japanese Navy vs The Allies New Guinea & the Solomons 1942-1944 (Avonmore Books, 2020)

Pacific Adversaries Volume Four: Imperial Japanese Navy vs The Allies -The Solomons 1943-1944 (Avonmore Books, 2021)

Pacific Profiles Volume One Japanese Army Fighters – New Guinea & the Solomons 1942-1944 (Avonmore Books, 2020)

Pacific Profiles Volume Two Japanese Army Bombers, Transports & Miscellaneous Types New Guinea & the Solomons 1942-1944 (Avonmore Books, 2020)

Pacific Profiles Volume Three Allied Medium Bombers: Douglas A-20 Havoc Series Southwest Pacific 1942-1944 (Avonmore Books, 2021)

Pacific Profiles Volume Four Allied Fighters: Vought F4U Corsair Series Solomons Theatre 1943-1944 (Avonmore Books, 2021)

South Pacific Air War Volume 1: The Fall of Rabaul December 1941–March 1942 (with Peter Ingman, Avonmore Books, 2017)

South Pacific Air War Volume 2: The Struggle for Moresby March–April 1942 (with Peter Ingman, Avonmore Books, 2018)

South Pacific Air War Volume 3: Coral Sea & Aftermath May–June 1942 (with Peter Ingman, Avonmore Books, 2019)

South Pacific Air War Volume 4: Buna & Milne Bay June – September 1942 (with Peter Ingman, Avonmore Books, 2020)

Introduction

Over a two year period from January 1942 to February 1944, land-based Zeros in the South Pacific (referred to as the "South Seas" theatre by the Japanese) waged a series of massive aerial battles both offensive and defensive in nature. Ultimately it was overpowering Allied resources which expelled Imperial Japanese Navy (IJN) air units from the Solomons and then Rabaul. Thousands of airmen had perished by the time a decision was made in Tokyo to relocate Rabaul's remaining air units to Truk in February 1944. By this stage a giant combined onslaught of USAAF, USN, RAAF, USMC and RNZAF units was pummelling Rabaul daily.

Many units staged throughout the theatre, and in November 1942 there was a restructure of IJN air power. This was mainly administrative in nature, however some units such as the Tainan *Ku* were recalled to Japan for reformation. Rabaul remained a hub for operations, and most Zero pilots served there at some stage in their careers. Given this background, the world of Zero markings in the South Seas area is predictably both complex and diverse. The research undertaken for this volume addresses many previous knowledge gaps, however the more discerning Zero aficionado will quickly ascertain that gaps still exist, particularly the issues raised in Chapter 13 pertaining to the *Rabauru Kokubuntai*.

The operational doctrine of the IJN stated that the rank of officer pilots should be indicated on their fighters. The policy arose as it was deemed critical that flight leaders be quickly identified during combat, however this ambitious requirement was enforced more by some units than others. The interpretation, structure and application of unit markings was decided in the field, and authorised at commander level. Unit colours were decided at *chutai* level, and each *chutaicho* usually took their colours with them as they transferred between units. If there were a conflict of colours, seniority held sway in deciding matters. Thus some *chutai* changed colours during their deployments, for example within the Tainan *Ku* when it transited from the Netherlands East Indies to New Guinea. Markings were applied according to the rules of the new unit into which they were assigned. In addition, some units were allocated to different parent *Koku Sentai* resulting in further markings changes.

All IJN aerial units based their operations and procedures around nautical concepts and procedures, and some heraldry flows from these. IJN rank structure was steadfast and strictly observed. Rank-consciousness is routinely borne out even in group photos: characteristically the most senior officer is usually seated in the wicker chair, surrounded by his favourite acolytes. Not all lieutenants (or other ranks) were equal. Seniority based on the graduation year from Eta Jima Naval Academy was also a key component of rank. So, two lieutenants in the same unit held differing seniority depending on when they graduated. Understanding these dynamics sometimes explains subtle markings vagaries, once again particularly in the case of the Tainan *Ku*.

Tail codes and other markings were often dictated by the units' *Koku Sentai* association. However, it is essential to understand the difference between *Koku Sentai* (Air Flotilla) and *Kushu Butai* translated as Attack Force. The former were commands based on administrative structure, whereas the latter were tactical operational formations.

Early Zeros – No Argument

It is unclear why debate still occurs over the green-grey colour of Zeros. This has been well-established in the past two decades by examination of extant pristine samples collected during the war, protected from the elements since, and also from post-war wreckage. The Japanese term "ameiro" is often connected with this colour, however this term originally arose from the concept that the colour resulted from a caramel-coloured varnish applied over neutral grey paint, which was never the case. The official colour term was "J3", but this is problematic because officially J3 was neutral-grey. It appears likely the grey/green colour resulted from the paint manufacturing process.

Every Zero wreck examined by the author in New Guinea and the Solomons has had the same and consistent green-grey overall paint application reflected in the profiles. Both Mitsubishi and Nakajima painted their Zeros in a semi-gloss olive-grey colour, the closest equivalent being FS 24201. Designed by Mitsubishi, by the beginning of 1942 Nakajima was also involved in the construction of the A6M Zero-sen series. There are minor differences between the markings of the two factory versions of this aircraft. The paint was sprayed over a dull red primer on the entire exterior surface with three exceptions: the cowling was painted a semi-gloss dark purple/black, for the early models the spinner was finished with a glossy aluminium paint and fabric ancillary control surfaces were painted with a semi-gloss medium grey (FS 26314). Many smaller components were painted by brush. The red used for stencils was equivalent to FS 21136. The yellow leading edge identification stripe which began to be applied in late 1942 resembles FS 23538, however Rabaul's hybrid paint stocks ensured variations on this theme. The blue used to indicate oleo overload markings was close to FS 25080, while undercarriage wells on Nakajima-built Zeros and some other interior components were painted in the striking translucent green protective coating the Japanese termed blue/green bamboo ("*aotake*"). Mitsubishi-built Zeros had undercarriage wells painted in the same olive grey paint as the rest of the aircraft. Most steel components were painted gloss black.

Caveats and Confusions

This volume only deals with land-based units. Note that many carrier-based units were also deployed to Rabaul or forward Bougainville airfields at various times for different campaigns (see Figure 1). Even though these carrier units were briefly land-based, their heraldry at first shared few markings principals with their land-based cousins. This explains why markings of some of Rabaul's land-based units have been much misrepresented over the years; some of these carrier-based Zeros have been portrayed and captioned as land-based and vice-versa. A good example is the Zeros from *Hiyo* during Operation I-Go which sported a contrasting two-tone camouflage, often misrepresented as a land-based scheme. Another is the No. 582 *Ku* Zeros with their distinctive chevrons, described wrongly in both Western and Japanese publications as assigned to the *Zuikaku*. Regrettably, these myths and other falsehoods continue to be perpetrated.

Which Model?

Relentless combat and bombing attacks put a premium on aircraft serviceability. Spares were often hard to source, and like their Allied counterparts, Japanese engineers through necessity often cannibalised parts from other airframes. This resulted in a suite of hybrid modifications, the most ubiquitous of which pertain to the Model 52 series. These late models were omnipresent at Rabaul from October 1943 onwards, and attendant field modifications offer the potential to confuse model numbers. Mitsubishi-constructed Model 52s from MN 3904 to 4007 left the factory with A6M3 cowl/collector/exhaust systems, and not the individual exhaust stubs which hallmark the later Model 52. Given the paucity of spares in the field, several early Model 52s and even a handful of Model 22s were retro-fitted with multiple-stack exhaust stub systems. Similarly, other similar engine, exhaust/collector, aerial and spinner changes were made in the field, confusing the issue in some cases of determining the particular model of a Zero. There is the additional factor of armament modifications of which unfortunately scant detail survives. For example, Admiral Kusaka Junichi's diary refers to the No. 204 *Ku* weapons testing centre not far from Vunakanau at which it unsuccessfully trialled, *inter alia*, the use of 30mm aerial cannon. Aerials can be another source of confusion. Some were removed entirely, others were switched, and some later models had a shortened version.

Markings Instructions

Markings changes for all South Seas fighter units were promulgated on 27 August 1943 which ordered that:

> Due to the possibility of being misidentified as enemy aircraft during combat, all fighters assigned to Southeast Area Operations will paint out any white outlines appearing on *hinomaru*.

This explains the dark green/black surrounds on many Rabaul's Zeros which previously had a white surround *hinomaru*.

Another paint scheme modification was the introduction of yellow leading edges for identification purposes (Identification Friend or Foe in Allied terms). However, as with all such orders, these took time to implement. The order was directed by the Minister for the Navy, Shimada Shigetaro, and dated 21 August 1942. Instructions were that the inner half of the leading edges of wings would be painted yellow for all camouflaged aircraft. The agreement became a joint one with the Imperial Japanese Army and the markings were ordered to be completed by 5 October 1942. However, the width of these yellow bands varied considerably, with Nos. 252 and 582 *Ku* having some of the widest.

Conclusions

Caution is in order for victory markings, or more to the point in the case of the IJN, the lack of them. The mindset of the IJN aviator was altruism, a philosophy of battle embodying sacrifice for the Emperor and Japan. Such credos leaves little room for individualism, and accordingly extraordinary feats were rarely recognised by individual acclaim. Many victory claims were shared in unit reports. Thus there was no practice of applying individual kill markings to unit aircraft, the only documented exception is contained in the memoirs of Warrant Officer Iwamoto Tetsuzo (see Profile 79). However it is important to note that no photo of Iwamoto's Zero has surfaced.

It would be nice if IJN markings regimes had remained orderly throughout the conflict, however the situation was anything but! Japanese fondness and observance of order are both reflected in the design of the markings systems, however orders of battle were often interrupted. High attrition rates meant fighters were assigned on the day to non-officer ranks on the basis of availability. Fighters were transferred, traded and borrowed between units. Legacy markings were painted over, or sometimes remained extant. Numbering systems went out of kilter, were abandoned under duress, or were renumbered for short-term expediency. In the heat of battle conditions, markings orders were modified, disobeyed or ignored. At the end of the day the South Pacific Zeros fought for their life. As such, their concern for future historians to describe and replicate orderly heraldry was understandably given a distant second consideration to fighting a war.

When they first arrived, Rabaul's Zero units were reasonably integrous before being badly broken up by the exigencies of combat and sent forwards to isolated bases in New Guinea and Bougainville. At lower rank levels, fighters were flown according to the day's roster. A *chutaicho* fighter, normally flown by an officer, could be borrowed by a lower ranking Warrant Officer or even a Petty Officer were he leading the day's formation, and vice versa. Thus for non-officer pilots it is wrong to claim that a particular fighter was assigned to or regularly flown by a particular pilot. The key example is the oft-published photo allegedly of FPO1c Nishizawa Hiroyoshi flying No. 251 *Ku* Zero tail code U1-105. This was not Nishizawa's assigned fighter; it is simply the one he was rostered to fly that day, and even that is unsubstantiated as we shall see.

As individual units became worn down through combat, extant systems of combat assignments became more stretched, and markings systems crumbled or became more *ad hoc*. Thus it would be possible for a *chutaicho* to borrow a *shotaicho* aircraft for a particular mission if no *chutaicho*-marked fighter was available. To a lesser degree, fighters were also redistributed between units (as happened during Operation I-Go), were assigned in from carrier groups or even borrowed from other units. Camouflage schemes varied considerably. They could be applied on top of extant schemes, both factory and field applied, and were applied by a variety of methods including paint-soaked cloth, spray gun or paint brush using varying pressures and distance settings. The only limitation on such schemes was the artistic license of the relevant painter. Low quality enamel paints applied in the field for camouflage purposes were quickly subject to the harsh weathering of the tropical environment. Neither did such inferior enamels grip steadfastly to the hardy "amerio" polyurethane semi-gloss used by Mitsubishi and Nakajima.

The South Seas' climate was brutal on airframes, meaning that debating precise colours is a semantic exercise. The colours of a brand new Zero, once subjected to the sun, heat and humidity of the Solomons, quickly and appreciably faded and desaturated. The end result varies on the scale from a neat and shiny new fighter through to extreme weathering patterns which complicated extant and random camouflage schemes. Perhaps the phrase "ordered chaos" best surmises the markings of Rabaul's manifold and various fighter units. Nonetheless, the Japanese tried to make order out of all this, making sense of which has proved challenging.

I hope you enjoy the conclusions of this lifetime pursuit. Let's hope these colourful South Seas Zeros will continue to fly for many years to come.

Michael Claringbould
Canberra, Australia, April 2021

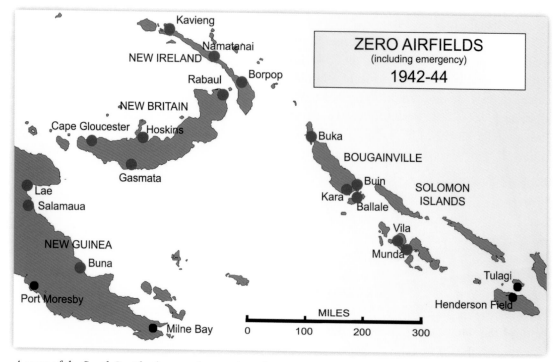

A map of the South Pacific theatre of operations (known as the South Seas theatre to the Japanese), showing airfields (red dots) used by Zeros. Black dots depict key Allied locations.

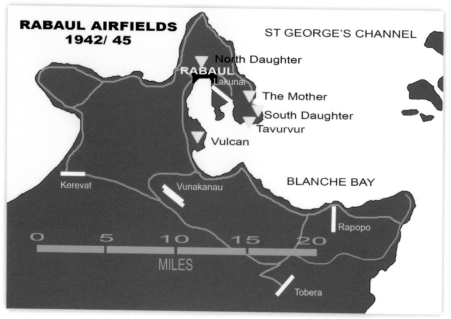

After occupying Rabaul in January 1942, the Japanese possessed two Australian-built airfields at Lakunai and Vunakanau both of which underwent much expansion during 1942-43. Located between an active volcano (Tavurvur) and the harbour Lakunai was mainly used as a fighter strip, while the more expansive Vunakanau became the main regional bomber base. Three other fighter strips at Kerevat, Rapopo and Tobera were constructed in 1943. Kerevat was mainly used for maintenance purposes.

Technical Notes:
Zero models in the South Seas

As the Solomons campaign increasingly encroached upon Rabaul, it became clear that the A6M2 Model 21 Zero fighter had fallen behind its US counterparts. A new generation of American fighters such as the P-38 Lightning and F4U Corsair, followed by the F6F Hellcat, possessed superior armament and high-altitude performance. However, the one advantage the Zero never conceded was its manoeuvrability at lower speeds.

Throughout early 1942, Nakajima continued to develop the original Model 12 Sakae engine installed in the A6M2. The resultant upgraded Sakae 21 incorporated a two-stage supercharger which required remodelling of the cowling and forward fuselage. However, a commensurate reduction in fuel capacity also reduced the range, exacerbated by the fact that the more powerful new radial also consumed more fuel.

The next Zero off the production line was the A6M3 Model 32 with square wingtips, and a reduced the wingspan to increase the high-speed roll rate. At the request of Rabaul's land-based units, the 20mm wing cannons had their magazine capacity raised to 100 rounds per weapon. This model first entered service in New Guinea in August 1942, however the curtailed range soon proved a disappointment in this tough theatre. Rabaul's reaction was to request an increase in fuel capacity, and this resulted in the A6M3 Model 22. The first fifty Model 22s assigned to the South Seas starting in February 1943 were also equipped with the Mk II long-barrel 20mm cannon.

Some Rabaul-based units used the Model 22 exclusively, a good example being No. 251 *Kokutai*. It received brand new Model 22s on which to train in Japan in early 1943. Due to the "hit and run" tactics employed by the new generation Allied fighters, in early 1943 Rabaul requested more firepower for the Zero, preferably with an improved rate of fire. However, Rabaul's own armament modifications and experiments near Vunakanau airfield saw no field modifications implemented in the Zero.

Meanwhile back in Japan around mid-1943 modifications had been considered on how speed and armament could be improved, resulting in the Model 52 with its shorter wingspan with rounded wingtips. The wing chord skin thickness was increased enabling a maximum diving speed of 410 miles per hour. The Sakae 21 engine was retained, and the new model was designated the A6M5 Model 52. With its shorter wingspan, the first Model 52 was delivered to Rabaul in September 1943, just over a month after this final model of the Zero had gone into production in August 1943. Mitsubishi made continual adjustments to the Model 52 airframe including thicker wing skins, pilot protection and armament changes to the cannon. All alterations incur compromise, and these modifications added considerable weight to the airframe resulting in less manoeuvrability.

Meanwhile in the South Seas front line, relentless attrition from combat and Allied bombing raids placed fighter serviceability in jeopardy. Spares became scarce, and engineers through necessity often cannibalised parts from other airframes. Despite the introduction of the Model 22 and 52 series Zeros, the Model 21 remained ubiquitous throughout, although it was rarely, if ever, seen in the inventories of Nos. 251 and 253 *Ku*. The Model 21 also remained almost ubiquitous to the carrier units which fought alongside Rabaul's land-based units.

Zero operations could extend to 30,000 feet, sometimes higher, and combats which developed into widespread engagements required good communication. However, radios were notoriously ineffective in all model Zeros, exacerbated by hot tropical conditions and poor shielding and grounding. Restricted transmissions saw exasperated IJN engineers remove most radio equipment, depending on the model, leaving Zero pilots to revert to the old way of hand signals for communication. Thus, a lack of command control plagued Zero operations around Rabaul and in the Solomons throughout the conflict.

Airframe Stencils

These airframe stencils are provided by Ryan Toews from his extensive study of Zero airframes over the years.

Note that the IJN required that all airframes be identified and both Mitsubishi and then Nakajima in November 1941 applied stencils to the rear port fuselage. The Nakajima identification stencil had a slightly different appearance to the Mitsubishi one and measured 250mm high by 330mm wide.

In October 1942 the IJN ordered that the date of manufacture was no longer to be indicated on the airframe. To comply with this order, both manufacturers left this section of the stencil blank on all airframes to leave the factory. In November of 1942, the IJN also revised the nomenclature for the Zero. The Type Zero Mark 1 Carrier-based Fighter Model 2 was henceforth to be known as the Type Zero Carrier-based Fighter Model 21.

FUSELAGE STENCILS

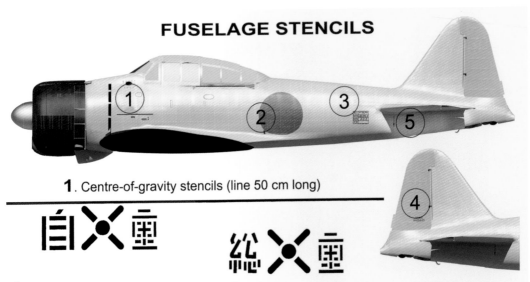

1. Centre-of-gravity stencils (line 50 cm long)

2. Port wing (indicates retractable step)

3. Manufacturer's stencils
(Mitsubishi)

Type	型式	零式一号艦上戦闘機 二型	Type Zero Mk I Carrier-based Fighter Model 2
Serial number	製造番號	三菱第1575號	Mitsubishi 1575
Date of Manufacture	製造年月日	2 - 2 - 9	9 February 1942
Assignment	所屬		

4. Nakajima number stencil
(starboard fin only)

零式艦戦
中島6546号

5. 'Support Here'

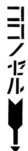

(Nakajima)

型式	零式一號艦上戦闘機一型	Type Zero Carrier-based Fighter Model 21
製造番號	中島第5359號	Nakajima 5359
製造年月日	2 - 10 - 23	23 October 1942
所屬		

WING & SPINNER STENCILS

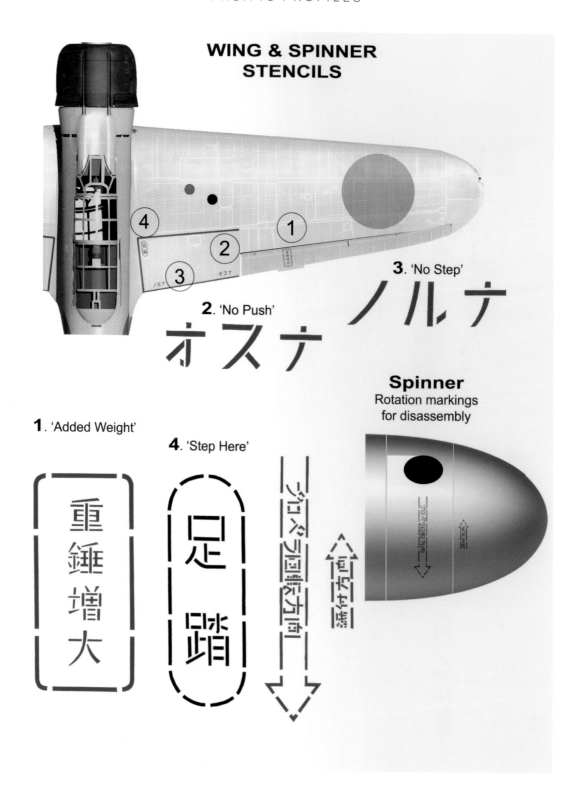

3. 'No Step'

ノルナ

2. 'No Push'

オスナ

Spinner
Rotation markings
for disassembly

1. 'Added Weight'

重錘増大

4. 'Step Here'

足踏

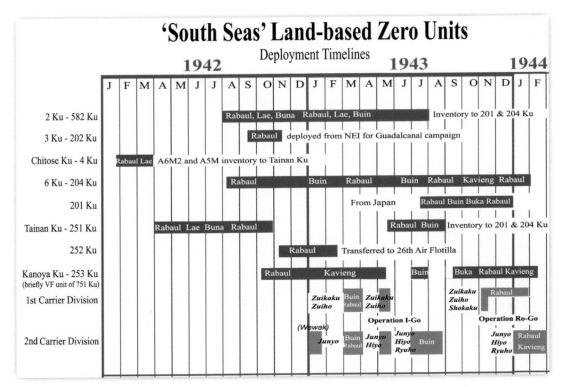

A diagram showing the deployment of land-based Zero units to the South Seas theatre during 1942-44.

A No. 4 Ku Model 21 Zero takes on a No. 75 Squadron, RAAF, Kittyhawk over Lae in March 1942.

Glossary & Abbreviations

Buntai	Equivalent to a *chutai*, but normally having an administrative or command status
Buntaicho	Leader of a *buntai*
Chutai	An aircraft formation which normally comprised a strength of nine aircraft. IJN fighter and bomber units normally had between three to five *chutai* with a Headquarters detachment.
Chutaicho	A Japanese flight leader of officer rank who commands a *chutai*
FCPO	Flying Chief Petty Officer (IJN)
Flyer1c	Aviator first class (IJN)
FPO1c	Flying Petty Officer first class (IJN)
FPO2c	Flying Petty Officer second class (IJN)
FPO3c	Flying Petty Officer third class (IJN)
Hikotaicho	Operational commander of a *kokutai*, one rank under a *hikocho*
Hikocho	Administrative and overall commander of a *kokutai*, superior in rank to a *hikotaicho*
Hinomaru	The red disc on the Japanese flag representing the sun and also used as a roundel on Japanese aircraft.
Hokoku	Inscriptions (translating as "service to the country") which signified that an aircraft was donated by an individual, organisation or corporation. This was IJN usage, as the JAAF equivalent was *Aikoku* meaning "love of country" or "patriotism".
IJN	Imperial Japanese Navy
Kodochosho	Japanese unit operations log
Koku Sentai	An Air Flotilla, the parent unit to several *Kokutai*
Kokutai	An IJN air group, consisting of between three to six *chutai*
Kushu Butai	Attack Force. Note that whereas *Koku Sentai* retained administrative command of units assigned to them, *Kushu Butai* were assembled as operational formations for a specific purpose. Thus a *Kushu Butai* could have various *Kokutai* within its formation from different *Koku Sentai*. To make matters more complex, some fighter units in the Solomons were occasionally reassigned within both *Kushu Butai* or *Koku Sentai*.

Ku	abbreviation of *kokutai*
Lieutenant (jg)	Lieutenant (junior grade)
MN	Manufacturer's Number
NEI	Netherlands East Indies
NHK	*Nippon Hoso Kyōkai* (Japan Broadcasting Corporation)
RAAF	Royal Australian Air Force
Rabauru Kokubuntai	Rabaul Air Force
RNZAF	Royal New Zealand Air Force
Shotai	A Japanese term defining an IJN flight, usually of three aircraft, however later in the theatre such flights often comprised four aircraft, especially within No. 204 *Ku*.
Shotaicho	Flight leader of a *shotai*
The Slot	A colloquial term, used by the Allies, referring to the NW/SE geographic ocean route which lay within the Solomon Islands.
US	United States
USAAF	United States Army Air Force
USMC	United States Marine Corps
USN	United States Navy
VMO-	Prefix for USMC Observation squadron, unusually in the case of VMO-251 which actually operated fighters from Guadalcanal.
VF-	prefix for USN Fighter Squadron

Note: Japanese terms are in *italics*. Also note that all Japanese names which appear in the text follow the Japanese format of surnames first.

The distinctive calligraphy of the prefix Q is showcased in this colour photo.

The intact airframe of Q-104 as captured at Buna, the subject of Profile 3.

CHAPTER 1
No. 2 *Kokutai*

Formed in Yokosuka as a mixed land-based dive-bomber and fighter unit headed by *hikocho* Commander Yamamoto Sakae, 15 Model 32 Zeros assigned to the No. 2 *Ku* fighter wing arrived in Simpson Harbour, Rabaul, on 6 August 1942 aboard the carrier *Unyo*. They were then flown off the carrier to Lakunai airfield.

The *buntaicho* of the fighter wing was Lieutenant Kurakane Yoshio who led all 15 on its first mission the very next day on 7 August 1942. This was flown in conjunction with Tainan *Ku* Zeros in a defensive attack against B-17 *Why Don't We Do this More Often* flown by Lieutenant Harl Pease, later awarded the Medal of Honor. Kurakane subsequently took nine Zeros to Buna on 22 August 1942, while the rest stayed behind at Rabaul. His first target from Buna was Milne Bay. The limited range of the Model 32s meant the unit did not participate in the early Guadalcanal campaign, but instead confined its operations to the New Guinea theatre, often flown alongside the Tainan *Ku*.

Unit Markings

At Buna, the Kurakane fighter detachment lost seven of its original fighter allotment to either aerial combat or Allied strafing and bombing attacks. Several wrecks abandoned there fortunately provide a detailed study of the unit's markings. On 28 September 1942, the entire fighter wing advanced to Buka with 21 fighters, reflecting an increased inventory which had been replenished with replacement Model 32s and possibly some Model 21s.

All of the original fighter complement of Model 32s were *Hokoku* aircraft, donated by patriotic organisations or individuals. All donations from HK-870 through HK-878, and possibly some either side of the range, were Korean donations. Accurate translation of these donor names has not occurred previously, largely due to the Korean language factor. These are correctly translated here for the first time.

The Combined Fleet ordered that both the Zeros and the Val dive-bomber contingents of No. 2 *Ku* were allocated the prefix "Q". The initial batch of Model 32s received tail codes Q-101 to Q-115, applied with red with white piping which has been confirmed via wartime colour photography of wrecks taken at Buna. The small Zero inventory meant there was only one *chutai*, and replacement aircraft were allocated new tail codes from where the previous ones left off.

Initially chevron markings on the fuselage were used to indicate *buntaicho* (double red chevrons) and *shotaicho* (single red chevron) aircraft. Tail stripes were not used, meaning that No. 2 *Ku* employed a basic heraldry system similar to that used by No. 4 *Ku*. Q-101 had a double chevron, while Q-103, Q-106, Q-109, Q-112 and Q-115 all had single ones. The unusual curly tail featured in the prefix "Q" was a unique design, and its origins are unknown.

The *chutaicho* Zero Q-101 later became tail code 2181 when the unit became No. 582 *Ku* (both numeral 1s on 2181 appear original, whereas the 2 and 8 are hand-painted over the previous Q-101 markings - see Profile 84 in the chapter on No. 582 *Ku*).

Around September 1942 the single red chevron was adopted as the unit marking, and thus subsequently applied to all aircraft. Ten additional Model 32s were delivered to Lakunai on 11 September 1942, bringing unit strength up to 18 Model 32s, and Q-122 was part of this delivery. The unit then advanced to Buka on 28 September 1942 with 21 aircraft after receiving a further three Zeros, most likely more Model 32s.

On 1 November 1942 as part of the IJN restructure, No. 2 *Ku* was renamed No. 582 *Ku*. No. 2 *Ku* and its successor No. 582 *Ku* were the only units to use the chevron marking in the South Seas theatre. This distinctive marking would later change colour to yellow just prior to the commencement of Operation I-Go in April 1943, on aircraft which had field-applied green upper surfaces.

Q-104 as captured at Buna, the subject of Profile 3, with several panels already souvenired by US soldiers.

The intact airframe of Q-102 as captured at Buna, the subject of Profile 2

Q-122 departing Lakunai, the subject of Profile 7. The twin in the background is J1N1 Irving tail code V-2 serving with the Tainan Kokutai.

A No. 2 Ku Model 32 at Lakunai.

No. 2 *Kokutai*

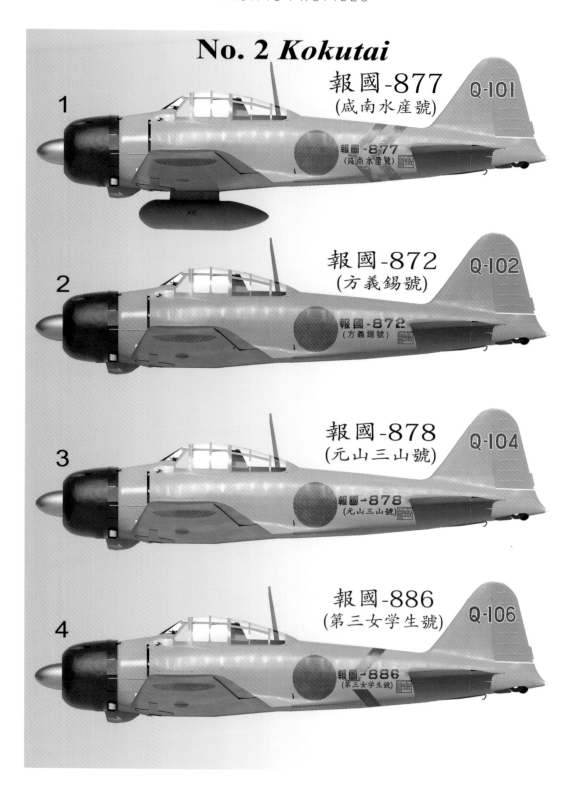

1 — 報國-877 （咸南水産號） Q-IOI
報國-877 （咸南水産號）

2 — 報國-872 （方義錫號） Q-IO2
報國-872 （方義錫號）

3 — 報國-878 （元山三山號） Q-IO4
報國-878 （元山三山號）

4 — 報國-886 （第三女学生號） Q-IO6
報國-886 （第三女学生號）

Profile 1: Mitsubishi A6M3 Model 32 MN 3035, Q-101, HK-877, Buna, August 1942, Lieutenant Kurakane Yoshio 倉兼義男.

The subscript for HK-877 translates as Hungnam Fisheries. Kannan is the Japanese pronunciation of the port on Korea's eastern coast named Hungnam, in South Hamgyong Province, North Korea. This Model 32 was completed on 6 July 1942 and assigned to *buntaicho* Lieutenant Kurakane Yoshio. It later received the re-applied No. 582 *Ku* tail code 2181 but was finally destroyed and abandoned at Lae.

Profile 2: Mitsubishi A6M3 Model 32 MN 3030, Q-102, HK-872, abandoned Buna 26 August 1942, Warrant Officer Tsunoda Kazuo 角田和男.

This Model 32 was completed on 30 June 1942 and abandoned at Buna following damage incurred during a dogfight with Airacobras on 26 August 1942 when flown by Warrant Officer Tsunoda Kazuo. The *hokoku* subscript indicates it was donated by Bang Uiseok, a Korean businessman.

Profile 3: Mitsubishi A6M3 Model 32 MN 3036, Q-104, HK-878, abandoned Buna, August 1942.

The *hokoku* subscript first shows Genzan, the Japanese pronunciation of Wonsan, a city in North Korea, followed by Samsan-dong, a neighbourhood in this city. Samsan literally translates as "three mountains". HK-878 was completed on 7 July 1942 and donated by the residents of Samsan. It too was abandoned at Buna after being damaged on the ground in an air raid.

Profile 4: Mitsubishi A6M3 Model 32 MN 3044, Q-106, HK-886.

The *hokoku* subscript translates as "3rd Women Students", and illustrated here for the first time, the *hokoku* subscript indicates this Zero was the third donated aircraft from the students of the National Women's Vocational School. The subscript is confirmed from a wartime *hokoku* postcard, and the airframe was completed on an unknown date in July 1942.

No. 2 *Kokutai*

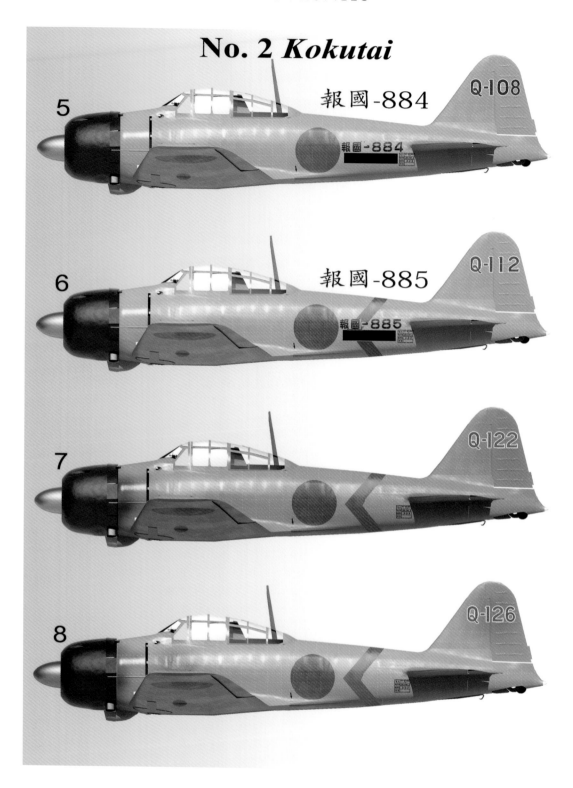

5   報國-884   Q-108

報國-884

6   報國-885   Q-112

報國-885

7   Q-122

8   Q-126

Profile 5: Mitsubishi A6M3 Model 32 MN 3042, Q-108,
HK-884 (unknown subscript), destroyed Buna, August 1942.

This was another Model 32 airframe abandoned at Buna. The subscript for HK-884 represents an unknown donor.

Profile 6: Mitsubishi A6M3 Model 32 MN 3043, Q-112,
HK-885 (unknown subscript), abandoned Buna, August 1942.

Illustrated for the first time, Q-112 was another airframe abandoned at Buna, with an unknown donor name. Wreck photos show this aircraft had a single red chevron as a *shotaicho* marking. "Q-112" was also hand-painted on the drop tank fairing.

Profiles 7 & 8: Mitsubishi A6M3 Model 32s, Q-122 and Q-126, Rabaul, September 1942.

These two Model 32s were among a batch of ten additional Model 32s delivered to the theatre on 11 September 1942. From around this time the chevron indicates assignment to No. 2 *Ku* and is not a *shotaicho* marking. Profile 7 is referenced from the photo on page 21 of the fighter taking off from Lakunai.

The subject of Profile 12 at Lakunai with the over-painted previous markings

The hokoku transcription on the starboard fuselage of X-168 as it lay in Guadalcanal jungle, the subject of Profile 14.

CHAPTER 2
No. 3 *Kokutai*

No. 3 *Ku* has an illustrious history, having been at the vanguard of the Japanese conquest of the Philippines and the Netherlands East Indies (NEI) in the first three months of the Pacific War. From bases in the NEI the long-range capability of its Zeros enabled No. 3 *Ku* to escort bomber raids over the northern Australian town of Darwin between March and August of 1942.

In order to reinforce Japanese air power for the Guadalcanal campaign, two *chutai* of No. 3 *Ku* Zeros were shipped from the NEI to Kavieng aboard the carrier *Taiyo*, arriving on 17 September 1942. This detachment comprised 26 pilots, 21 Model 21 Zeros (two full *chutai* plus three spares) and four C5M Babs reconnaissance aircraft. *Hikocho* Lieutenant-Commander Sakakibara Kiyoji commanded the detachment. The No. 1 *chutai* (red fuselage band) was commanded by Lieutenant Aioi Takahide who also served as the detachment's *hikotaicho*, and the No. 2 *chutai* (yellow fuselage band) was led by Lieutenant (jg) Yamaguchi Sadao.

After arriving at Kavieng, the detachment took several days to transfer to Lakunai, Rabaul, from where it flew its first combat mission on 22 September. Its operations were placed under the command of the Tainan Ku, which at the time also incorporated the No. 2 chutai in its operations. The unit was renamed No. 202 Ku on 1 November, however unit markings were not changed until after the unit returned to the NEI. The detachment served nearly seven weeks in New Guinea and the Solomons, and after seeing considerable action and losses, its pilots withdrew from Rabaul on 8 November 1942 whilst their surviving mounts were distributed among the Tainan *Ku* inventory.

The fuselage and tail stripe markings system used by No. 3 *Ku* evolved from that used in China by No. 12 *Ku*, the first IJN unit to use the Zero. Many former members of No. 12 *Ku* were later transferred into No. 3 *Ku* when it was established in 1941, and these transferees took the markings system with them. No. 3 *Ku* indicated *chutaicho* rank with two fuselage bands and two tail stripes, a *shotaicho* with one band and two stripes, and all other fighters with one band and one stripe. Fuselage colours were initially No. 1 *chutai* red (X-101 to X-118), No. 2 *chutai* blue (X-121 to X-129), white (X-141 to X-149), yellow (X-161 to X-169) and black (X-181 to X-189) with these number ranges later expanding. It is possible that *shotai* colors were white, blue, red and black, however white for No. 1 *shotai* appears confirmed from photos. The two detachments sent to Rabaul appeared to have broken from this pattern, adopting the *shotai* colour to match the *chutai* colour. Several *chutaicho* came and went during the unit's first year, possibly changing *chutai* colours and markings models, which might account for these differences. The unit was originally established with six *chutai*, adding to the complexity of matters. A lack of photographs to more closely scrutinise the topic and establish adequate data points does not help.

No. 3 *Kokutai*
South Seas Detachment, Aioi *Chutai*

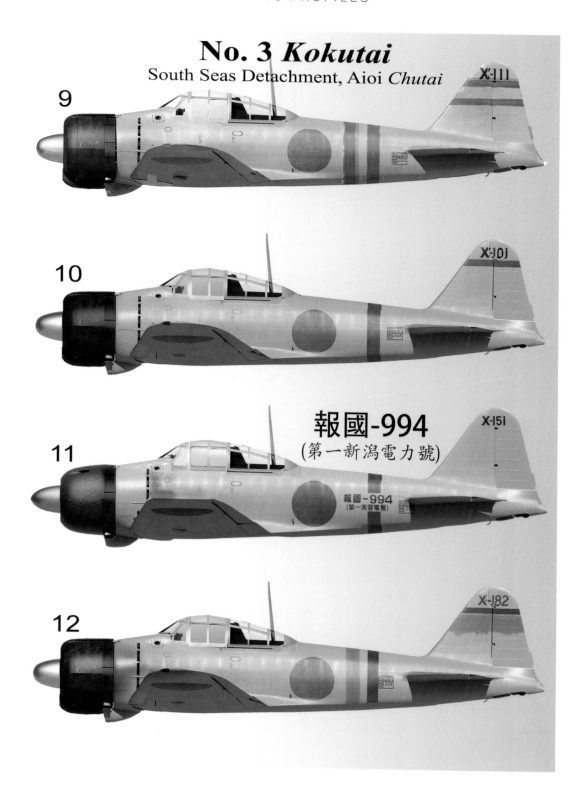

9

X-111

10

X-101

報國-994
(第一新潟電力號)

11

X-151

報國-994
(第一美音電髮)

12

X-182

Profile 9: Mitsubishi A6M2 Model 21, X-111,

hikotaicho Lieutenant Aioi Takahide 相生喬秀, October 1942.

Referenced from a photo taken at Lakunai in October 1942, Lieutenant Aioi Takahide's *chutaicho* position is indicated by two fuselage stripes. This profile and Profile 10 are based on a personally annotated photo of both Hashiguchi Yoshiro and Aioi researched by Japanese markings authority Nick Millman. The *kodochosho* shows that Hashiguchi often flew in Aioi's *shotai*.

Profile 10: Mitsubishi A6M2 Model 21, X-101,

FPO2c Hashiguchi Yoshiro 橋口嘉郎, September 1942.

Often flown by Hashiguchi, this Model 21 was photographed at Lakunai in September 1942. It was one of four Zeros claimed by VF-5 Wildcat pilots over Guadalcanal on 27 September 1942 when flown by Hashiguchi, positioned as wingman to *hikotaicho* Lieutenant Aioi Takahide. On this day 17 No. 3 *Ku* Zeros joined a full *chutai* of Tainan *Ku* Zeros to escort Bettys down The Slot. Hashiguchi survived the encounter, however.

Profile 11: Mitsubishi A6M3 Model 32, X-151, FPO1c Ito Kiyoshi 伊藤清, October 1942.

This Model 32 served with No. 3 *Ku* around the time of the Rabaul deployment however it is not confirmed that it was sent to Rabaul. The *hokoku* subscript indicates the fighter was the first donation by the Niigata Electric Power Company, and the fighter was often flown by FPO1c Ito Kyoshi. The donor's name is correctly illustrated for the first time, referencing naming ceremony invitation documents.

Profile 12: Mitsubishi A6M2 Model 21, X-182, Lakunai, October 1942.

This Model 21 was photographed at Rabaul. The painted-over *chutaicho* fuselage band and tail stripe on the fin have erased the black fuselage band and white tail stripe markings of previous *chutaicho* Lieutenant Miyano Zenjiro who left No. 3 *Ku* in April 1942.

No. 3 *Kokutai*
South Seas Detachment, Yamaguchi *Chutai*

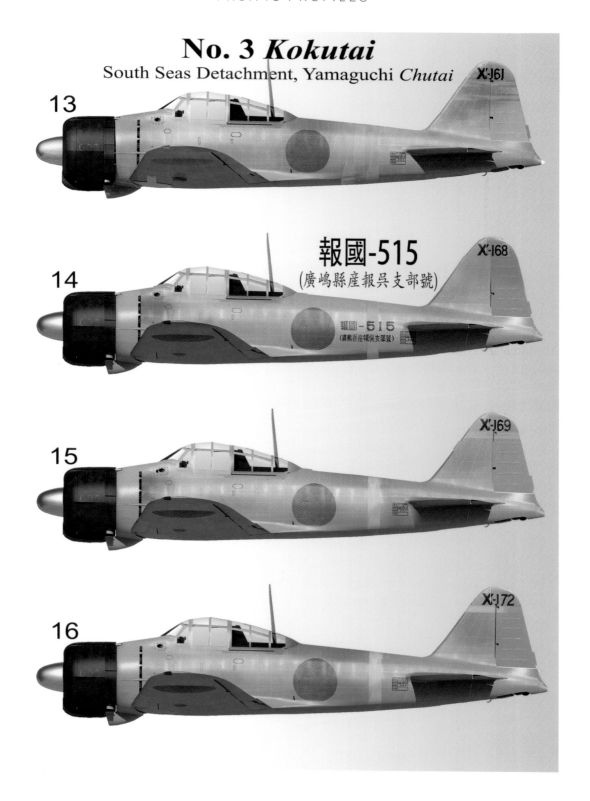

13

X-161

14

報國-515

(廣嶋縣産報呉支部號)

X-168

15

X-169

16

X-172

Profile 13: Mitsubishi A6M2 Model 21, X-161, No. 2 *chutai chutaicho*

Lieutenant Yamaguchi Sadao 山口定央, October 1942.

Photographed at Lakunai during the deployment, the twin yellow fuselage bands on this Model 21 denote Yamaguchi's *chutaicho* status.

Profile 14: Mitsubishi A6M2 Model 21 MN 2666, X-168, HK-515,

force-landed Guadalcanal late 1942.

The subscript on HK-515 translates as the Kure Chapter of the Hiroshima Commercial Trade Association Patriotic Society. During the war this society was a nation-wide organisation with its headquarters in Kure, and several branch offices including the one at Hiroshima. The society closed in September 1945. The markings for this fighter are sourced from colour photos of the aircraft post-war where it forced-landed on Guadalcanal. The fin was destroyed in the crash however, and it might have had a *shotaicho* stripe. The aircraft was completed at the factory on 31 March 1942 and was forced-landed during the Rabaul deployment by an unidentified No. 3 *Ku* pilot who was later returned to Rabaul by destroyer.

Profiles 15 & 16: A6M2 Model 21s X-169 & X-172.

Both these *shotaicho* Zeros were photographed at Lakunai during the deployment.

The hokoku transcription and data stencil showing MN 2666 on the port fuselage of X-168 in Guadalcanal jungle, the subject of Profile 14.

A USN photographer stands on the relic of a No. 4 Ku Zero at Lae in October 1943. In the background can be seen shotaicho airframe F-151, the subject of Profile 22.

The narrow and unique calligraphy of No. 4 Ku tail codes on display. This is the remains of F-115, the subject of Profile 21.

CHAPTER 3
No. 4 *Kokutai* (Fighter Wing)

No. 4 *Ku* was a composite fighter and land-attack bomber unit formed on 10 February 1942 at Rabaul. The fighter wing was amalgamated from the Okamoto *chutai* of the Chitose *Ku* based at Truk, and the Kawai *chutai* detachment of the Tainan *Ku* based at Palau. It operated only two types of fighter - the Mitsubishi A5M4 Claude and Model 21 Zero.

The fighter wing's aerial actions span only a brief two months. No. 4 *Ku* Zeros mostly fought RAAF Hudsons, Catalinas and Kittyhawks. This is particularly significant as the wing constituted the first adversaries to the Kittyhawks assigned to No.75 Squadron, RAAF, which was the very first fighter unit to defend Port Moresby. Many sources erroneously attribute the Kittyhawks' opponents as Tainan *Ku* Zeros, whereas most of the conflicts were with No. 4 *Ku*.

As *buntaicho*, Lieutenant Okamoto Harutoshi brought a wealth of operational and leadership experience. He had flown combat missions in China, from carriers, and had previously acted as *buntaicho* of the Kasumigaura *Ku*. He was appointed in September 1941 as *buntaicho* for the Chitose *Ku* fighter wing, and arrived in Truk a month later where his leadership made its mark. He led the No. 4 *Ku* fighter wing on both its inaugural landmark missions against Port Moresby on 24 and 28 February 1942. Okamoto was recalled to Japan when the wing was incorporated into the Tainan *Ku* in April 1942, however he later returned to the South Pacific theatre in late 1943 to take up the position of *buntaicho* of No. 253 *Ku*.

Of 39 pilots who served with the No. 4 *Ku* fighter wing, only six would survive the war, including Okamoto. The majority lost their lives in 1942 after being assimilated into the Tainan *Ku* in April of that year.

Unit markings

As increasing numbers of Zeros were assigned into the unit at Rabaul, the Claudes were relegated to daily patrols over Rabaul, while the more potent Zeros were kept for alerts and offensive missions. The pilots from the Kawai *chutai* (Lieutenant Kawai Shiro) arrived at Rabaul onboard the *Meiten Maru* on 25 January 1942, along with the first three A6M2 Zeros to arrive at Rabaul. The modest shipment, possibly tail codes S-143, S-144 and S-145, was distributed to the Okamoto *chutai* for operational purposes although they retained Kawai *chutai* markings. The Zeros, which took several days to assemble and test fly, had previously been used as trainers in the Marshall Islands. They became F-143, F-144 and F-145 respectively.

The next Zeros to appear in Rabaul were ten Model 21s delivered by the aircraft carrier *Shoho* on 17 February 1942, including several Nakajima-built Zeros (MNs 16, 17, 18, 19, 910 and 911). Two of these, MNs 16 and 18 were later captured derelict at Lae in September 1943. All of these were allocated Okamoto *chutai* tail codes in the F-107 to F-116 range, the earlier range of F-101 to F-106 already allocated to the A5M4 inventory.

No fuselage band was assigned to indicate assignment to the parent Air Flotilla, and the marking instead indicated *chutaicho* and *shotaicho* status; one band denotes a *shotaicho*, two bands a *chutaicho*. The colour of these bands signals the *chutai* to which they were assigned. During its brief life until assimilated with the Tainan *Ku* in April 1942, the wing operated a total of 15 A5M4 Claudes and 32 A6M2 Model 21 Zeros.

Several key photographic references survive from the many No. 4 *Ku* airframes left derelict at Lae. The Okamoto *chutai* sported black fuselage bands, and was allocated six A5M4s and ten Zeros, tail codes F-101 through F-116. It is reasonably sure that the Iwasaki *chutai* used red, as No. 75 Squadron Kittyhawk pilots reported engaging Zeros with red fuselage bands over Port Moresby in March 1942. Its allocated strength of six A5M4s and eleven Zeros used tail codes F-120 through F-136. The Kawai *chutai* applied yellow bands and was allocated three A5M4s and eleven Zeros with tail codes F-140 through F-153.

A shipment of replacement Zeros was sent to No. 4 *Ku* which arrived in early April 1942, and so these were probably given Tainan *Ku* markings. By studying the pattern and calligraphy of tail codes in both the No. 4 and Tainan *Ku*, one can ascertain those Zeros which were No. 4 *Ku* hand-me-downs among Tainan *Ku* losses. No. 4 *Ku* used unique calligraphy for the numeral "5" - with a lower curvature at the bottom of the numeral. It also used a distinctive thinner and elongated "4". Discerning between No. 4 *Ku* and Tainan *Ku* fonts, even from black and white photos of relatively poor quality, is thus relatively straightforward.

During the 1 April 1942 IJN restructure, the Tainan *Ku* adopted, rebuilt and expanded No. 4 *Ku*'s *chutai* structure and aircraft strength. It did this by replacing lost A6M2s with new aircraft, and recycled the former tail codes of the lost aircraft. Examples are V-110, V-134 and V-152, as replacements for F-110 (derelict at Lae shortly after receiving tail code V-110 and Tainan *Ku* markings), and F-134 and F-152 (lost in combat or due to accidents).

The No. 4 *Ku* tail prefix "F" was replaced by the Tainan Ku prefix "V". Examples are V-108, V-136 and V-153, previously F-108, F-136 and F-153 (Kawai's Zero). Then, when sufficient numbers of A6M2 replacements arrived, A5M4s were purged from the Tainan *Ku* inventory and their tail codes recycled onto replacement Zeros; e.g. Tainan *Ku* codes V-103 and V-104 were tail codes formerly applied to A5M4s F-103 and F-104.

There are sufficient data points to demonstrate that markings application was systematic in both No. 4 *Ku* and Tainan *Ku*. Every third fighter was a *shotaicho* aircraft; the markings of all three *chutai* conform to this pattern. The first tail code assigned to the Okamoto *chutai* was F-101, with *shotaicho* marked as F-103 (A5M4), F-106 (A5M4), F-109 (A6M2 - assigned to FPO1c Oshima Toru), F-112 and F-115, the *chutaicho* fighter assigned to *hikotaicho* Okamoto Harutoshi. The same pattern applies to the other two *chutai*, starting at tail codes F-120 and F-140 respectively.

The elongated unique style of calligraphy on V-136 indicates this was previously No. 4 Ku's F-136.

The remains of the Kawai chutai's F-146.

A full perspective of shotaicho airframe F-151, the subject of Profile 22.

Allied intelligence surveyed a sufficient number of No. 4 Ku airframes at the former No. 4 Ku base at Lae from which to reconstruct the definitive structure of tail codes used within the unit.

No. 4 *Kokutai*
Iwasaki *Chutai*

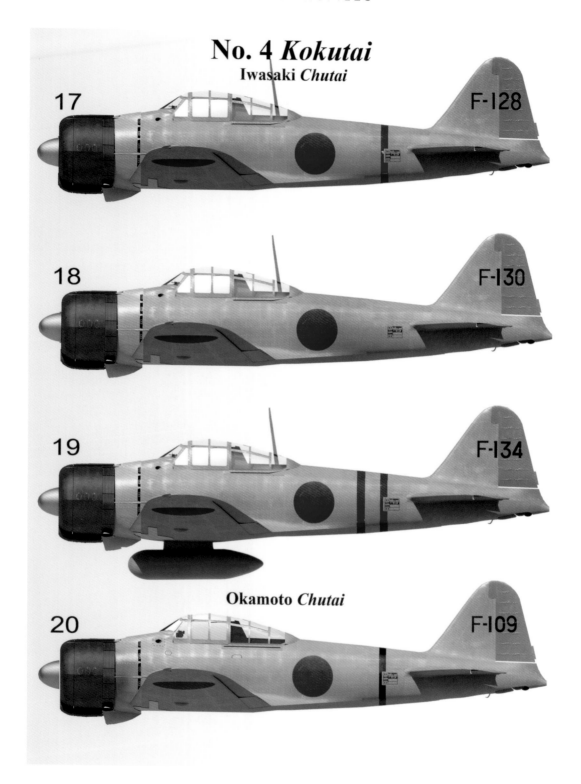

17   F-128

18   F-130

19   F-134

Okamoto *Chutai*

20   F-109

Profile 17: Mitsubishi A6M2 Model 21, MN 644, F-128.

This *shotaicho* airframe later became *shotaicho* fighter V-128 with the Tainan *Ku* (see Profile 39), and it is sometimes claimed that this was flown by FPO1c Sakai Saburo.

Profile 18: Nakajima A6M2 Model 21, MN 646, F-130.

This airframe became V-130 with the Tainan *Ku* (see Profile 40). While strafing an airfield at Milne Bay on 27 August 1942 it was hit by AA fire. The pilot, FPO2c Kakimoto Enji, ditched into the bay and was captured.

Profile 19: Mitsubishi A6M2 Model 21, MN 4443, F-134,

buntaicho Lieutenant (jg) Iwasaki Nobuhiro 岩崎信廣.

This fighter was shot down over Horn Island on 14 March 1942, and a visiting Air Technical Intelligence Unit team noted the tail markings included the numeral "4" (the body and identification discs of Lieutenant Iwasaki Nobuhiro were retrieved a year later). F-134 was the *chutaicho* fighter of the Iwasaki *chutai*. Subsequent to his loss, others acted in Iwasaki's place as *chutaicho* including FPO1c Nishizawa Hiroyoshi and FPO1c Oshima Toru. It is likely they operated *shotaicho*-marked aircraft in doing so.

Profile 20: Nakajima-built A6M2 Model 21, F-109, *shotaicho* FPO1c Nishizawa Hiroyoshi

西澤広義, Rabaul, March 1942.

The single black fuselage band on this Zero denotes a *shotaicho*, and F-109 was flown by FPO1c Nishizawa Hiroyoshi in the early days of No. 4 *Ku* at Rabaul, before the unit was divided into *chutai* (F-109 was subsequently allocated to the Okamoto *chutai*).

No. 4 *Kokutai*
Okamoto *Chutai*

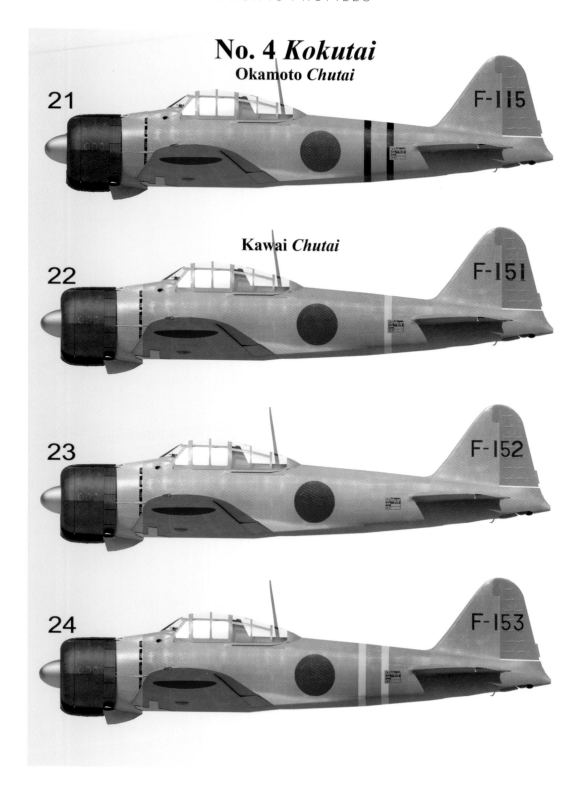

21   F-115

Kawai *Chutai*

22   F-151

23   F-152

24   F-153

Profile 21: Nakajima-built A6M2 Model 21, F-115, *hikotaicho* Lieutenant Okamoto Harutoshi 岡本晴年, destroyed on ground at Lae, 22 March 1942.

F-115 was destroyed by No. 75 Squadron Kittyhawks on 22 March 1942 during a strafing attack against Lae. Photos of the airframe subsequent to its capture exhibit the two black *buntaicho* stripes.

Profile 22: Mitsubishi A6M2 Model 21, MN 4438, F-151.

This *shotaicho* Model 21 was destroyed on the ground at Lae, date unknown.

Profile 23: Mitsubishi A6M2 Model 21, MN 5439, F-152.

FPO3c Kikuchi Keiji forced-landed at Lae after engaging No. 32 Squadron Hudsons near Lae on 22 March 1942 and was likely flying this fighter at the time. This assessment derives from photos at Lae taken after its capture which clearly show that V-152 was marked with a thick tail font, characteristic of replacement Zeros assigned into the Tainan *Ku*. This indicates that V-152 was a replacement airframe, indicating that F-152 was likely lost while in No. 4 *Ku* service.

Profile 24: Mitsubishi A6M2 Model 21, F-153 (later V-153), *chutaicho* Lieutenant Kawai Shiro 河合四郎.

This Model 21 was an older version, fitted with external mass balance arms on the ailerons.

This painting of U-163 departing Lakunai in October 1942 was made by an artist on the ground and is published in No. 6 Ku's unofficial history.

CHAPTER 4
No. 6 *Kokutai*

No. 6 *Ku* was formed at Kisarazu, Japan in April 1942, and by August the unit was scheduled to occupy to the new airfield at Lunga Point, Guadalcanal. However, these plans were scuttled when the Americans captured the field. Instead, No. 6 *Ku* was quickly ordered to reinforce Rabaul.

Hikocho Morita Chisato decided to only include experienced pilots in the advance detachment to Rabaul. This was led by Lieutenant Kofukuda Mitsugu who took 18 Model 32 Zeros to Lakunai, Rabaul, where they all arrived safely on 21 August 1942. Guided by two G4M1 bombers, they flew via Iwo Jima, Saipan and Truk in a landmark long distance navigation feat for IJN fighters. Following a week of maintenance and familiarisation flights, Kofukuda organised a series of patrols from Rabaul the first of which involved nine Zeros on 1 September. This advance detachment was also involved in attacks against Milne Bay and in a substantive combined strike against Port Moresby on 6 September.

Meanwhile the main body which had initially been left behind in Japan arrived at Rabaul on 7 October aboard the carrier *Zuiho*. Led by Lieutenant Miyano Zenjiro, this reinforcement of 27 Zeros comprised a mixture of Model 21s and 32s. At Rabaul, Miyano made plans to move his contingent to Buka on Bougainville. The first patrol from Buka was made on 8 October by Zero tail codes U-158 and U-164 together with *shotaicho* FPO1c Okazaki Seiki flying U-167.

Over the next few days the strength at Buka was brought up to two dozen Zeros before the unit commenced combat operations. Even though the weather was poor, on 11 October 21 Zeros conducted four separate staggered patrols from Buka to cover warships which were bombarding Guadalcanal. The marginal weather cost five aircraft. Three pilots were rescued after ditchings however two experienced pilots, *chutaicho* Lieutenant Kuba Kazuto and *shotaicho* Warrant Officer Sagane Isahito, failed to return. On 15 October, Miyano's contingent at Buka redeployed southwards to Buin, brought back up to a strength of two dozen airframes since the loss of the five aircraft on 11 October.

As part of the IJN restructure of 1 November 1942, No. 6 *Ku* was renamed No. 204 *Ku* whilst retaining the same leadership structure.

Unit markings

No. 6 *Ku* was allocated the tail code prefix "U" when it was formed on 1 April 1942. Although few photos of No. 6 *Ku* Zeros were taken in the South Seas, there are several artistic and photographic references in the unofficial history of No. 6/204 *Ku* published by the unit's veterans after the war.

The diary of FPO1c Murakami Keijizo shows that his Model 32 had the tailcode U-107 when he ditched on 11 September 1942. Photos show that these early Model 32 airframes remained uncamouflaged, at least for the first few weeks of service. This suggests that the tail codes of Kofukuda's advanced detachment were numbered U-101 to U-118. Other references suggest that Miyano's follow-on detachment was numbered U-131 upwards. It is possible that a third *chutai*, led by *chutaicho* Lieutenant Kuba Kazuto, was then formed, with tail codes commencing at U-151. However, as described above, Kuba was lost on 11 October and it is likely his pilots were then incorporated into Miyano's *chutai*. Nonetheless the operational structure of No. 6 *Ku* and its markings from October 1942 onwards are both uncertain. Around late October the unit started field camouflaging its airframes in both random splotch patterns and overall green. Following the application of camouflage, tail codes were repainted in white to facilitate their visibility. Nonetheless, the unit's markings remain unclear, particularly in respect to *chutaicho* and *shotaicho* airframes.

This photo of No. 6 Ku Zeros, captioned as near Rabaul, was published in Japanese magazines in 1943. However, the censor has removed the tail codes. Note also that the front and second-most fighter appear to be the same aircraft from a different perspective, suggesting that the photo is a doctored composite. A thin line is discernible in both chutaicho stripes.

This photo, also captioned as near Rabaul, appears to be from the same sequence as the photo on page 42 and also has tail codes removed. Two of the Zeros appear to have double dark chutaicho stripes, either red or black, suggesting these are associated with either the Miyano or Kuba chutai. More examples of No. 6 Ku's early camouflage scheme showcase how random these schemes were.

Shotaicho FPO1c Okazaki Seiki flies U-167 on the first patrol mission from Buka on 8 October 1942.

No. 6 *Kokutai*

25

U-107

26

U-131

27

U-167

28

U-163

Profile 25: Mitsubishi A6M3 Model 32 U-107.

FPO1c Murakami Keijizo ditched near Kitava Island 11 September 1942.

Profile 26: Nakajima A6M2 Model 21 U-131, *chutaicho* Lieutenant Miyano Zenjiro 宮野善次郎, Buin, October 1942.

This profile is sourced from a photo taken near Rabaul in late 1942 which appears to depict No. 6 *Ku* Model 21 Zeros (see the photo on page 42). Unusually the two *chutaicho* stripes (portrayed as yellow but could be blue) have a narrow band within them, either red or black. The tail code U-131 is speculative based on the possibility that Miyano's *chutai* codes began at U-131.

Profile 27: Mitsubishi A6M2 Model 21 U-167, Buka, 8 October 1942.

No. 6 *Ku*'s operations log shows that *shotaicho* FPO1c Okazaki Seiki flew this Zero from Buka on 8 October 1942. This Zero, part of the Kuba *chutai*, was likely to have a single *shotaicho* stripe.

Profile 28: Mitsubishi A6M3 Model 32 U-163.

A painting of this fighter with this tail code appears in the unofficial history of No. 6/204 *Ku* written by veterans (as shown on page 40). The background palm trees suggest the location was Lakunai. The changeover from No. 6 *Ku* to No. 204 *Ku* did not occur until 1 November 1942, when the unit was based at Buin, thus the camouflage would have been applied when the fighter was still serving with No. 6 *Ku*.

The subject of Profile 31 taxies at Lakunai.

CHAPTER 5
Kanoya *Kokutai*

The Kanoya *Ku* was established as a land-attack unit equipped with G4M1 Bettys, however on 1 April 1942 a decision was made to attach a fighter wing to the unit. The new detachment originally became the No. 3 *chutai* and was assembled at Don Muang airfield, north of Bangkok. Lieutenant Ito Toshitaka was appointed *chutaicho*, subordinate to *hikocho* Lieutenant Commander Tamai Asa'ichi.

For its first six months the Kanoya *Ku* fighter wing trained in Malaya until it was ordered to Rabaul following the American invasion of Guadalcanal. The wing arrived at Kavieng on 19 September 1942 before flying the following day to Rabaul. On 21 September Lieutenant Ito led nine Kanoya *Ku* Model 21 Zeros as participants in a substantive strike against Port Moresby with other IJN units. The Kanoya *Ku* fighters were tasked with escorting eight G4M1s (less one which aborted) of the Kanoya's No. 1 *chutai*, a long return flight of more than five hours to Port Moresby from Rabaul.

In October 1942 more replacements bolstered the wing's strength to two dozen Model 21s. On 1 November 1942, commensurate with the IJN restructure, the unit was redesignated as the No. 253 *Ku*. Commander Kobayashi Yoshito was appointed *hikotaicho* and the new *kokutai* had its authorised strength increased to 48 fighters and four Ki-46 reconnaissance aircraft. These latter four aircraft arrived in February 1943 and were shared in operations with No. 204 *Ku*. Attached to the 21st Air Flotilla and first based at Kavieng, No. 253 *Ku* detachments subsequently saw service throughout most South Seas bases (see Chapter 11).

Unit Markings

The Kanoya *Ku* fighter wing's Model 21s remained in factory finish, and until the 1 November 1942 restructuring the units in the Southwestern Area Fleet (encompassing Thailand and Malaya) used red tail codes. Kanoya *Ku* tail codes commenced with K-101 and it is likely that K-101 was the *buntaicho* aircraft although this is still unsubstantiated. Photos of the unit's Zeros are hard to find given its limited time in combat of around six weeks before becoming No. 253 *Ku*.

Kanoya *Kokutai*

29 K-112

30 K-125

報國-556
(第三水産千葉號)

31 K-108

報國-556
(第三水産千葉號)

32 K-128

Profile 29: Nakajima A6M2 Model 21 MN 3178, K-112, Rabaul, September 1942.

This Zero was photographed at Don Muang airfield, Bangkok, in August 1942. The MN 3178 was just visible on the rudder, indicating it was a Nakajima-built A6M2 made in late July 1942. Note that Nakajima Zeros had no white surround on the fuselage *hinomaru* until the very end of August 1942. K-112 was among the first batch of Zeros sent on the long ferry flight to Kavieng then on to Rabaul.

Profile 30: A6M2 Model 21 K-125.

This Model 21 was photographed at Penang around August 1942 and it is likely it was also delivered to the Southeastern Area theatre.

Profile 31: A6M2 Model 21 K-108, HK-556, MN 5649, Rabaul, October 1942.

The red fin stripe is a leadership marking, likely indicating a *shotaicho*. The subscript for HK-556 indicates this was the third aircraft donated by Chiba Fisheries.

Profile 32 : A6M2 Model 21 K-128, Rabaul, October 1942.

As above, the red fin stripe likely indicates a *shotaicho*. The tail code is speculative. It is based on the sequencing of tail codes which would have made K-128 a *shotaicho* mount.

The subject of Profile 41 as captured at Lae.

The subject of Profile 41 at Lae, extracted from a colour movie.

CHAPTER 6
Tainan *Kokutai*

Alongside No. 3 *Ku*, the Tainan *Ku* was heavily involved in operations in the first months of the Pacific War during the capture of the Philippines and the Netherlands East Indies. In April 1942 the unit was transferred to Rabaul where it absorbed the fighter wing of No. 4 *Ku*. Its Zeros were then balanced operationally between a defensive detachment at Rabaul and a forward-deployed echelon stationed at Lae on mainland New Guinea. In subsequent months the Tainan *Ku* saw intense combat with Allied aircraft based at Port Moresby, often on a daily basis, weather permitting. Largely from its impressive record during this period, the Tainan *Ku* is the most well-known Zero unit to serve in the South Seas theatre.

By August the unit commenced a deployment to Buna, which did not last long as the strategic situation quickly changed following the American invasion of Guadalcanal. Tainan *Ku* Zeros then began flying very long-range escort missions from Rabaul to Guadalcanal and suffered significant attrition. By end of October most of the unit's core of experienced pilots had been killed. Some returned to Japan, including the famous ace FPO1c Sakai Saburo. By the time of the November 1942 IJN restructure the unit had become a shadow of its former self, and although it received some replacement aircraft, it could not replace its experienced pilots.

Markings

The Tainan *Ku* markings system is the most complex of all the New Guinea IJN fighter units. This is due in no small part to the fact that its inventory was subject to constant attrition, it had adopted No. 4 *Ku*'s fighter inventory, and it operated fighter wings at both Lae and Buna which both had considerable autonomy. The operational structure of the Tainan *Ku* in New Guinea thus became flexible, driven by structural necessity and relentless attrition on both pilots and aircraft.

All of the unit's initial batches of Model 21s and those it inherited from No. 4 *Ku* were early production machines, with the original spinner design of shorter length and rounded tip. The unit reached its peak strength around May/June 1942, after which it was challenged to mount missions of more than two operational *chutai*. The understrength nature of the unit explains why, after arrival in New Guinea, it could field only three *chutai* (Nos. 1, 2 and 3 with colours red, blue and yellow), with No. 4 (black) added later. Previously in Bali, from whence it arrived in New Guinea, it had fielded five *chutai* out of an original six, one of which had been detached to the Philippines.

When the Tainan *Ku* arrived in New Guinea it incorporated the three *chutai* of No. 4 *Ku*, initially expanding the number of operational *chutai* to six. This was the same structure as the unit had in Bali, however for markings reasons only three *chutai* colours were used. Thus, we see the Kurihara and Yamashita *chutai* sharing the colour red, *et al*. A breakdown of the unit's operational logs shows the unit briefly operated eight *chutai* after Lieutenant Inano Kikuhito arrived at Rabaul. Later, three smaller *chutai* exclusively operating Model 32s were added, but short on promised airframes, the No. 4 (black) *chutai* was incomplete and it appears it only operated one aircraft (V-190).

The early markings breakdown of each *chutai* commencing in May 1942 was:

- V-101 to V-109: possibly led by Lieutenant (jg) Kurihara Katsumi, red, only one oblique stripe on V-108 to mark a *buntaicho* fighter;

- V-110 to V-118: Lieutenant Yamashita Joji, red, two stripes on the V-117 *buntaicho* aircraft;

- V-120 to V-128: Lieutenant (jg) Sasai Jun'ichi, blue, one stripe on the V-121 *buntaicho* aircraft;

- V-129 to V-137 (with V-138 added later): Lieutenant Commander Nakajima Tadashi, blue, two stripes on the V-138 *hikotaicho* aircraft;

- V-140 to V-148: yellow, one oblique yellow fuselage stripe and two red tail stripes on the V-147 *buntaicho* aircraft;

- V-149 to V-157: Lieutenant Kawai Shiro, yellow, two yellow oblique stripes and two black tail stripes on the V-153 *buntaicho* aircraft. The black tail stripes are an anomaly. It appears likely that Kawai, when based at Lae with No. 4 *Ku* before it was amalgamated with the Tainan *Ku*, surmised the new merged unit markings before the new Tainan leadership cadre arrived at Rabaul. Thus, he used the same unit colours he had used on his A6M2, tail code V-172, before his *chutai* was detached to Palau, and re-equipped with A5Ms.

- V-161 to V-169: black, one oblique stripe on the *buntaicho* aircraft;

- V-170 to V-178: Lieutenant Inano Kikuhito, black, two stripes on the V-177 *buntaicho* aircraft.

Once the Tainan *Ku* arrived in New Guinea they replaced the white with red piping "V" tail code to overall black. The codes were probably applied using stencils; an outline was traced in pencil then the numeral painted in with a brush. Pilots in rank-and-file positions did not have individual aircraft assigned, instead flying fighters allocated on the day.

When the Tainan *Ku* was amalgamated with the No. 4 *Ku* fighter wing on 1 April 1942, it was administratively allocated 45 aircraft. Given Japanese military efficiency, it is likely that the "V" tail code prefix as directed would have replaced the "F" prefix shortly thereafter, however exactly when this occurred is unclear. The initial administrative allocation of tail codes at Lae and Rabaul (and the colour of the oblique fuselage sash) was:

- V-101 through V-115 (18 aircraft*) red oblique stripe

- V-120 through V-135 (18 aircraft*) blue oblique stripe

- V-140 through V-155 (18 aircraft*) yellow oblique stripe

* each *chutai* had three aircraft allocated as spares, at least on paper, however they never materialised.

The rank conscious IJN incorporated a system of clear rank delineation in its markings, the only unit in New Guinea to do so. *Shotaicho* had one white, blue, red or black horizontal tail stripe above the "V" tail unit code indicating the position of No. 1, 2, 3 and 4 *shotaicho* respectively; *buntaicho* carried two tail stripes equally spaced above and below the tail code in the colour of the respective *shotai* to which the fighter was assigned. An example is Zero V-108 with only one fuselage stripe but two tail stripes, indicating likely assignment to a junior Lieutenant or even Warrant Officer. The reality was that due to combat losses, there was no luxury of maintaining the rigidity of such a definitive markings system, and it is unclear how this played out in practice. In addition, new leadership arrived at various junctures of the unit's deployment and this also played out in the markings policy. As attrition took its toll, by late July 1942 the Tainan's other *chutai* had expanded their tail code range thus;

- V-101 through V-119, red oblique stripe, No. 1 *chutai*

- V-120 through V-139, blue oblique stripe, No. 2 *chutai*

- V-140 through V-159, yellow oblique stripe, No. 3 *chutai*

- V-161 though V-179, black oblique stripe, No. 4 *chutai*

The Buna detachment formed its own rules, intending for a long-term deployment which was cut short after the failure of the Milne Bay invasion. The colour order of *shotaicho* stripes was the same, however three separate *chutai* were created specifically for the detachment with Nos. 1, 2 & 3 *chutai* having the colours of blue, yellow and black. It is possible that the black tail tip on V-177 is a variation on a *shotaicho* marking, however regardless this marking is unique to the Buna detachment. The planned markings structure which was never fulfilled was:

- No. 1 *chutai* V-170 - V-179: blue

- No. 2 *chutai* V-180 - V-189: yellow

- No. 3 *chutai* V-190 – V-199: black (it appears only V-190 was assigned)

Pilots rest under buntaicho Lieutenant Kawai Shiro's V-153 at Rabaul, the subject of Profile 37.

Commander Nakajima's Zero at Lakunai, the subject of Profile 43.

The Zero ditched by FPO2C Kakimoto Enji, the subject of Profile 40. Although unclear in this photo, the tail code V-130 was prominent on the fin along with the single blue stripe.

The hokoku script on Profile 47 as discovered at Buna.

The intact wreck of Profile 46 as discovered at Buna.

The wreck of V-110 as paraded in Sydney in 1943. This is the V-110 which replaced the one in Profile 35.

Tailcode II-111 of the 22nd Koku Sentai fighter wing is seen at Khota Baru, Malaya. This unit was comprised of one each detached chutai from the No. 3 and Tainan Ku. It appears likely the No.3 Ku Zeros were returned to No. 3 Ku with the Tainan Ku Zeros being taken over by No. 3 Ku or possibly the Kanoya Ku.

Tainan *Kokutai*
Kurihara *Chutai*

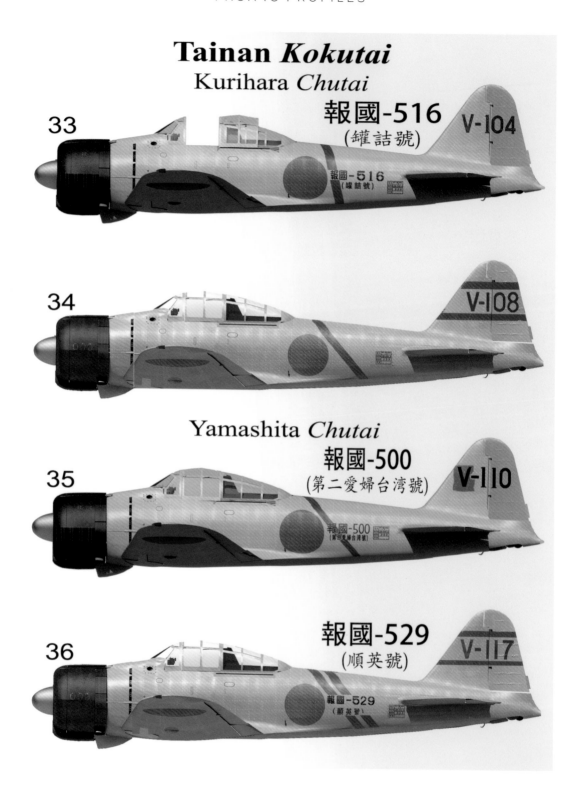

33 報國-516
(罐詰號)
V-104
報國-516
(罐詰號)

34 V-108

Yamashita *Chutai*

35 報國-500
(第二愛婦台湾號)
V-110
報國-500
(第二愛婦台湾號)

36 報國-529
(順英號)
V-117
報國-529
(順英號)

Profile 33: Mitsubishi A6M2 Model 21 MN 1640, V-104, HK-516, (possibly Kurihara *chutai*), Flyer1c Kawanishi Haruo 河西春男 , shot down Port Moresby, 2 May 1942.

Flyer1c Kawanishi Haruo was flying V-104 when shot down 16 miles from Port Moresby behind Porebada village by 8th Fighter Group P-39 pilot Donald McGee on 2 May 1942. Note that the oblique stripe was at an unorthodox steep angle.

Profile 34: Mitsubishi A6M2 Model 21 V-108, Kurihara *chutai*, assigned to *buntaicho* Lieutenant (jg) Kurihara Katsumi 粟原克美, abandoned at Lae.

The wreckage of this aircraft was photographed at Lae in September 1943. The two red tail stripes with a single fuselage stripe indicate that this fighter was shared by Lieutenant Yamashita Joji's two deputies, Warrant Officer Yamashita Sahei and Lieutenant (jg) Kurihara Katsumi.

Profile 35: Mitsubishi A6M2 Model 21, (possibly MN 5374), V-110 (previously F-110), HK-500, Yamashita *chutai*, operational loss Lae April 1942.

This Model 21 fighter was captured at Lae in September 1943 and preceded the later V-110 lost on 28 April 1942. The *hokoku* subscript indicates the 2nd Patriotic Women's Association of Taiwan. The calligraphy of the tail code is thinner than its replacement V-110, indicating this fighter previously served with the No. 4 *Ku* fighter wing.

Profile 36: Mitsubishi A6M2 Model 21 MN 2641, V-117, HK-529, Yamashita *chutai*, assigned to *buntaicho* Lieutenant Yamashita Joji 山下丈二, shot down at Rabi (Milne Bay) 27 August 1942.

Referenced to post-war colour photographs taken of its wreckage in New Guinea, the *hokoku* subtext indicates that the fighter was donated by Japanese citizen Shibuya Yoshihide, who also donated HK-1182 and at least one other aircraft to the Japanese war effort.

Tainan *Kokutai*
Kawai *Chutai*

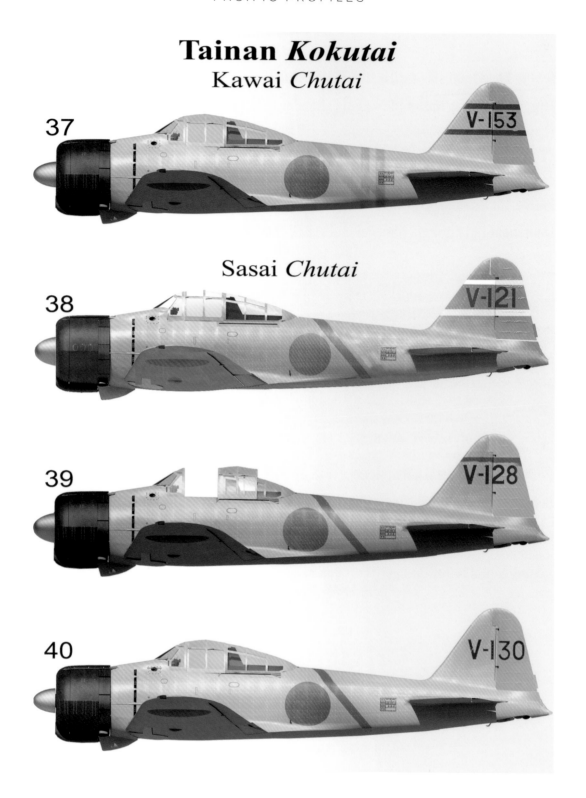

37

V-153

Sasai *Chutai*

38

V-121

39

V-128

40

V-130

Profile 37: Mitsubishi A6M2 Model 21 V-153 (previously F-153), Kawai *chutai*, *chutaicho* Lieutenant Kawai Shiro 河合四郎.

This was an early Model 21 with external mass balancers on the ailerons. It had previously served as *buntaicho* Lieutenant Kawai Shiro's aircraft at Lae, explaining the two over-painted No. 4 *Ku* vertical yellow fuselage stripes from its previous assignment. It appears Kawai painted the fin stripes in his pre-war unit colour of black before the Tainan *Ku* contingent arrived at Lae from Bali, unaware of plans for Tainan *Ku* markings structures in New Guinea.

Profile 38: Mitsubishi A6M2 Model 21 V-121, Sasai *chutai*, *buntaicho* Lieutenant (jg) Sasai Jun'ichi 笹井醇一, shot down Guadalcanal 26 August 1942.

Lieutenant (jg) Sasai Jun'ichi was flying this Zero when he was shot down over Henderson Field, Guadalcanal, on 26 August 1942 with the kill credited to a VMF-223 Wildcat flown by Captain Marion Carl. Note that as a junior officer, Sasai's fighter has only one single fuselage band and two tail stripes.

Profile 39: Nakajima A6M2 Model 21 MN 644, V-128 (previously F-128), Sasai *chutai*, shot down Milne Bay 27 August 1942 flown by FPO1c Yamashita Sadao.

Although no known photo exists of this aircraft, it is often claimed that FPO1c Sakai Saburo was flying this fighter on his final flight over Guadalcanal on 7 August 1942 after which he was repatriated to Japan with an eye injury. The tail code is allegedly sourced from Sakai's logbook, although the entry has never been made public. Furthermore, although this fighter is profiled incorrectly in numerous publications with a white tail stripe, V-128 bore a red one to denote its placement in the third *shotai*. This Zero was being flown by FPO1c Yamashita Sadao when he was shot down at Milne Bay on 27 August 1942 by No. 75 Squadron, RAAF, Kittyhawk pilots Squadron Leader Les Jackson and Sergeant Roy Riddel.

Profile 40: Nakajima A6M2 Model 21 MN 646, V-130 (previously F-130), Nakajima *chutai*, FPO2c Kakimoto Enji 柿本圓次, ditched at Milne Bay on 27 August 1942.

This fighter was retrieved and examined by Allied intelligence several weeks after it ditched, with the tail code confirmed from Allied intelligence reports.

Tainan *Kokutai*
Inano *Chutai*

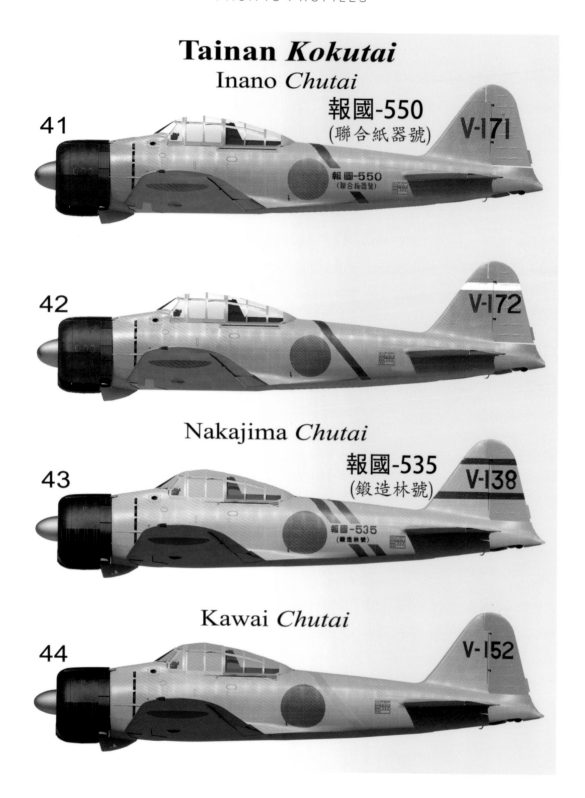

報國-550
(聯合紙器號)

V-171

41

報國-550
(聯合紙器號)

42

V-172

Nakajima *Chutai*

報國-535
(鍛造林號)

V-138

43

報國-535
(鍛造林號)

Kawai *Chutai*

V-152

44

Profile 41: Mitsubishi A6M2 Model 21 MN 5779, V-171, HK-550, Inano *chutai*.

Built by Mitsubishi on 30 May 1942, the donor was United Daily Newspaper Products. The aircraft was captured as a derelict at Lae in September 1943.

Profile 42: Mitsubishi A6M2 Model 21 MN 5784, V-172, No. 4 *chutai*.

Completed by Mitsubishi in May 1942, this Zero is presently on display at the Australian War Memorial (AWM), painted incorrectly with a blue sash and tailcode V-173. After the Tainan *Ku* was disbanded in November 1942, this fighter was transferred to No. 204 *Ku*. At time of publishing the AWM was considering repainting the Zero in the correct markings as seen here.

Profile 43: Mitsubishi A6M2 Model 21 MN 2776, V-138, HK-535, Nakajima *chutai*,
hikotaicho Lieutenant Commander Nakajima Tadashi 中島正.

This aircraft was photographed at Rabaul on 7 August 1942 and was assigned to *hikotaicho* Lieutenant Commander Nakajima Tadashi. The *hokoku* subscript represents the Hayashi Forging Co. Ltd, a steel forging manufacturing company headquartered in Hebei City, Ishikawa Prefecture, Japan. Note that the numeral "8" appears to have been applied using an upside-down stencil.

Profile 44: Mitsubishi A6M2 Model 21 V-152 (previously F-152), Kawai *chutai*.

Captured at Lae in September 1943 as an abandoned airframe, V-152 was first identified on Lae 'drome in a New Guinea Volunteer Rifles intelligence report dated 23 April 1942. It is likely that this fighter was written off by FPO3c Goto Tatsusuke on 17 April 1942 after being damaged by RAAF Kittyhawks near Port Moresby.

Tainan *Kokutai*
Buna Detachment

45   V-177

46   報國-870 （洪源號） V-187

47   報國-874 （定平號） V-190

Inano *Chutai*

48   報國-490 （阿波製紙號） V-179

Profile 45: Mitsubishi A6M3 Model 32 MN 3018, V-177, Buna detachment, assigned Lieutenant Inano Kikuhito 稲野菊一.

Completed by Mitsubishi on 15 June 1942, the black fin tip on this fighter is sourced to a colour photograph and is likely a variation *shotaicho* marking unique to the Buna detachment. This Zero was captured at Buna airfield on 27 December 1942 after the Battle of Buna, upside down and with flaps lowered.

Profile 46: A6M3 Model 32 MN 3028, V-187, HK-870 Buna detachment.

Built by Mitsubishi on 28 June 1942, the *hokoku* subscript indicates this Zero was donated by the citizens of Hongwon County, a county in South Hamgyong province, North Korea. Its derelict airframe was captured at Buna airfield on 27 December 1942. Note that the yellow fuselage sash has been painted snug around the *hokoku* calligraphy.

Profile 47: Mitsubishi A6M3 Model 32 MN 3032, V-190, HK-874, assigned Lieutenant Inano Kikuhito 稲野菊一, abandoned at Buna.

This fighter was the second assigned to Lieutenant Inano Kikuhito, when appointed *buntaicho* of the Buna detachment. Completed at Mitsubishi on 3 July 1942, the *hokoku* subscript shows this fighter was donated by the citizens of Chongpyong County, a county in South Hamgyong province, North Korea. The airframe was captured at Buna airfield on 27 December 1942, then subsequently disassembled and transported to Brisbane, where it was evaluated at Eagle Farm airfield for intelligence purposes.

Profile 48: Mitsubishi A6M2 Model 21 MN 4668, V-179, HK-490, No. 4 *chutai*.

Built by Mitsubishi on 14 April 1942, the fighter was donated by the Awa Paper Manufacturing Company, headquartered in Tokushima, Japan. The derelict airframe was documented by the Air Technical Intelligence Unit at Lae on 16 September 1943. Its MN indicates it was delivered to the unit around June 1942 and was replaced by another V-179.

CHAPTER 7
No. 201 *Kokutai*

Formed from the Chitose *Kokutai* in the Marshall Islands on 1 December 1942, No. 201 *Ku* left the Marshalls for Japan in February 1943, leaving their Zeros behind to be transferred to other units. In late June 1943 it was ordered to join the 21st *Koku Sentai* and allocated an authorised strength of 45 Zeros which, alongside 27 D3A2 Vals assigned to No. 552 *Ku*, were loaded aboard the carrier *Unyo* for delivery to Truk. Further aerial deliveries saw all No. 201 *Ku's* fighters arrive in the South Seas theatre by 15 July 1943, realising an inventory of 18 Model 22s and 42 Nakajima-built Model 21s.

No. 201 *Ku's* *hikocho* throughout its South Seas deployment was Commander Nakano Chujiro, with *hikotaicho* Lieutenant Kawai Shiro. This latter officer was a highly experienced veteran who had originally arrived in the New Guinea theatre in January 1942 as a *chutaicho* with the Chitose *Ku*. Kawai subsequently led No. 4 *Ku* until it was amalgamated into the Tainan *Ku* in April 1942.

By mid-July 1943 about half of No. 201 *Ku* had taken up station at Buin with 25 Zeros, flying their first combat mission on 21 July. This was a late afternoon sweep against Rendova of 15 Zeros led by Lieutenant Arai Tomoyoshi, flying in formations of four-fighter *shotai*, an operational practice recently instituted by No. 204 *Ku* which was also based in the Bougainville forward combat zone at this time. No enemy were encountered. Meanwhile, the rest of No. 201 *Ku* remained at Rabaul performing defence and convoy protection duties.

By October 1943, No. 204 *Ku* had suffered horrendous pilot losses due to combat, malaria and dengue fever. Accordingly, it was withdrawn from Bougainville operations on 8 October, leaving No. 201 *Ku* as the sole defenders of Buin. By this stage Allied air raids and attrition from combat had also depleted No. 201 *Ku's* Zero inventory and in late October its nine surviving airworthy fighters at Buin were flown to Buka while the entire ground echelon was evacuated back to Rabaul by sea. By the end of the month both Buin and Ballale were classified as unsuitable for fighter operations and both bases were effectively vacated by the aerial units, leaving behind only reduced garrisons. The unit was soon withdrawn entirely to Rabaul, led by Lieutenant Oba Yoshio, the only operational officer still alive following months of intense combat.

The largest combat fought by No. 201 *Ku* unfolded on the morning of 14 September 1943. The unit launched 20 Zeros alongside other Zero units in a series of sorties which at one time totalled 117 Zeros aloft to defend Buin from USAAF Liberators escorted by their own substantive fighter escort. From this combat, FCPO Okumura Takeo was awarded the highest number of kills for one mission for any IJN unit during the Pacific war: nine fighters and one bomber. The Japanese claimed a total of 60 kills for the day. However, the claims were fanciful given that the total American losses were only five aircraft. In turn, American claims were for 18 victories against five Japanese fighters actually downed. No. 201 *Ku* was withdrawn to Saipan in early January 1944 when it became clear it lacked sufficient resources to sustain combat operations.

Markings

Herewith the delivery list of A6M2 Zeros to No. 201 *Ku* from Nakajima by Manufacturer's Number from 26 March to 6 June 1943, totalling 75 new airframes: 6747, 5756, 5759, 4764, 4765, 3777, 3778, 3779, 2781, 2782, 2784, 2785, 2787, 2788, 2789, 1790, 1792, 1793, 1794, 1797, 1799, 1801, 1802, 9811, 9816, 8820, 8823, 8824, 7830, 6845, 5850, 5853, 4867, 3878, 3879, 2882, 2885, 1894, 1907, 1908, 1909, 9914, 8921, 8923, 8925, 8928, 8929, 6940, 6943, 6944, 5952, 5955, 4961, 3973, 3978, 2985, 2986, 2989, 1990, 1991, 1993, 1994, 1997, 1998, 11000, 11002, 11003, 11004, 11007, 91011, 91013, 71031, 71033, 71035 & 71038

No. 201 *Ku* was assigned to the 24th *Koku Sentai* and allocated the tail code prefix "W1". Its mixed inventory of Model 21 and 22 Zeros all sported green spinners. It also operated at least one G4M1 as a transport, with the tail code W1-901. The methodology of the unit's markings has not been established, although it is clear from the tail codes that the unit operated with three *chutai*. It appears that the Nos. 1, 2 and 3 *chutai* used the colours of red, yellow and white. *Shotaicho* aircraft were indicated by one stripe above the tail code, the colour of which might have changed depending on the *shotai* number (1, 2 or 3). At least one *chutaicho* aircraft, W1-165, had white diagonal wing markings. Some references link the prefix "6" with the unit's Zeros when they became part of the "Rabaul Air Force" (see chapter 13 and Profile 97), however this association is unconfirmed. Tail codes were applied in both white and yellow. Perhaps during the early part of its South Seas deployment white was first used and then yellow on subsequent airframes.

Model 21 Zero W1-111 in flight over Bougainville in July 1943, having just arrived in the South Seas theatre.

No. 201 *Kokutai*

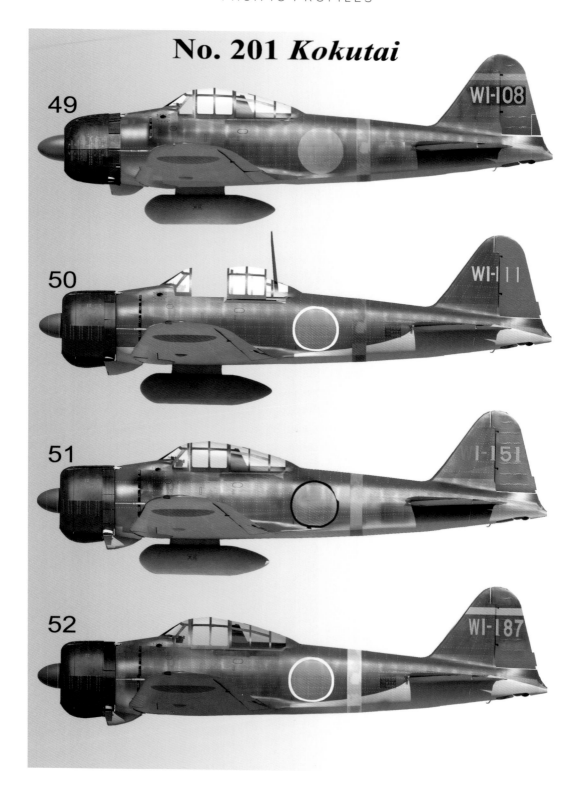

49

50

51

52

Profile 49: Mitsubishi A6M3 Model 22 W1-108,
shotaicho FCPO Okumura Takeo 奥村武夫 Buin, August 1943.

This aircraft is associated with *shotaicho* FCPO Okumura Takeo who is listed as flying a Model 22 with tail code W1-108. No photograph of this Zero is available so the markings are still speculative, however it is unlikely the "W1" prefix was still in use during the air battle over Buin on 14 September 1943.

Profile 50: Nakajima A6M2 Model 21 W1-111, Buin, July 1943.

This profile is referenced from a photo of the fighter in flight over Bougainville, showing the white-surround Nakajima *hinomaru* and aerial. Note the clear camouflage delineation of the factory-applied camouflage scheme.

Profile 51: Nakajima A6M2 Model 21 W1-151, Buin, July 1943.

This profile is referenced from a photo taken on the ground at Buin around July/August 1943. Note that the white piping on the *hinomaru* has been painted over in a dark green to lessen visibility. The letter "W" in the tail code was either worn or obscured by camouflage paint.

Profile 52: Nakajima A6M2 Model 21 W1-187, *shotaicho*, Buin, August 1943.

These markings are referenced from a wreck salvaged post-war from Bougainville. It had the original code W1-187 hand-painted in yellow, with a yellow *shotaicho* stripe above. The code 6-136 was later applied over this code, spraying it on using a stencil. The white fuselage band conforms to a No. 3 *chutai* airframe.

Model 21 Zero W1-151 at Buin in late 1943, alongside other Model 21s with "Rabaul Air Force" tail codes 2-131 and 6-135 (See Chapter 13). A detachment of No. 201 Ku moved to Bougainville after 15 July 1943, nominally under the control of the 26th Koku Sentai, however in reality this did not eventuate until the end of August. This ambiguity possibly explains why we see in this photo a representation of the W1 tail code alongside the numeric tail codes used by fighter elements within the 26th Koku Sentai.

Seen at Munda airfield in August 1943, the remnants of a painted-over fuselage band indicate the subject of Profile 54 was likely received from No. 252 Ku in February 1943.

The subject of Profile 60 captured at Vila field, Kolombangara. This aircraft was transferred to No. 204 Ku from No. 252 Ku at end of February 1943. Note the white piping added to the upper wing hinomaru.

CHAPTER 8
No. 204 *Kokutai*

No. 204 *Ku* saw the most extended and heaviest combat of any Zero unit in the South Seas theatre. Aside from being a stalwart in the Guadalcanal operation, it also played key roles in Operations I-Go and Ro-Go, the Rendova attacks and finally the defence of Rabaul. The unit's pilots also flew as escort to Admiral Yamamoto on the fateful mission on which he was lost on 18 April 1943.

During the IJN restructure of 1 November 1942, No. 6 *Ku* was redesignated No. 204 *Ku* and the unit tail code prefix was changed from "U" to "T2". The changeover date found the newly minted No. 204 *Ku* on the frontline base of Buin where *hikotaicho* Lieutenant Kofukuda Mitsugu continued to direct operations, mainly defensive patrols of Buin and Ballale, providing cover for Guadalcanal destroyer convoy runs and the occasional offensive fighter sweep. Kofukuda first arrived in theatre on 21 August 1942 (see Chapter 4), and soon his unit was operating a mixed inventory of Model 21, 22 and 32 Zeros. A change in command in March 1943 saw both the unit's *hikocho* and *hikotaicho* rotated back to Japan and replaced: *hikocho* Captain Morita Chisato was replaced by Captain Sugimoto Ushie, and Lieutenant Kofukuda was replaced by Lieutenant Miyano Zenjiro.

Sugimoto introduced new tactics and instituted regular training missions despite ongoing combat. *Hikotaicho* Miyano fitted some of his Zeros with 30-kilogram bombs. He tried them out unsuccessfully as fighter-bombers for the first and last time on 7 June 1943 against American ground positions in the Russell islands. That morning Miyano led two dozen Zeros from Buin, structured in three *chutai* alongside two dozen No. 251 *Ku* Zeros with Miyano's eight Zeros each toting two 30-kilogram bombs. These Zeros went in low but were met with heavy ground fire. They were also attacked by more than a hundred American fighters which cost No. 204 *Ku* three Zeros, including experienced *shotaicho* FCPO Hidaka Yoshimi. A fourth Zero was lost when it was force-landed by a wounded pilot.

A decisive mission for No. 204 *Ku* unfolded shortly thereafter on 16 June 1943, when Miyano led three *chutai* of two dozen Zeros structured into six four-aircraft *shotai*, tasked to protect two dozen No. 582 *Ku* Vals attacking Guadalcanal. However, the mission was a disaster: 13 Vals were shot down and No. 204 *Ku* lost four Zeros with three more pilots wounded, two seriously. The damage to morale was severe as those lost included *hikotaicho* Miyano himself and his trusted deputy *chutaicho* Lieutenant Morisaki Takeshi. This now rendered the unit without any officer pilots until the following month when Lieutenant Commander Shindo Saburo from No. 582 *Ku* was transferred across as the new *hikotaicho*.

To consolidate forces, in mid-July 1943 No. 204 *Ku* was amalgamated with the remnants of the depleted fighter wing of No. 582 *Ku*. Prior to this the No. 582 *Ku* fighter wing and No. 204 *Ku* were grouped together as the 6th Air Attack Force, an operational construct, and placed under the administrative umbrella of the 26th *Koku Sentai*. Curiously, the No. 582 *Ku* fighter wing was assigned to a different Air Attack Force than No. 582 *Ku*'s dive-bombers. Then at the end of August the Zero complements of the *Junyo* and the *Ryuho*, which had been brought into the Solomons in early July, operated alongside No. 204 *Ku*.

The ongoing pressures of mounting Allied air attacks subsequently saw No. 204 *Ku* retreat to Rabaul in October 1943 where it became a key defending unit against the Allied campaign to reduce the Japanese bastion. On 26 January 1944 No. 204 *Ku*'s remaining dozen battle-worn Zeros were withdrawn to Truk, with all surplus pilots transferred to No. 253 *Ku*.

Markings

The unit underwent two distinct markings phases. The first was when it replaced the previous No. 6 *Ku* tail codes with an unhyphenated black tail code beginning with the prefix T2 (see Profiles 53 and 54). When No. 204 *Ku* started applying green camouflage in the field, it switched placement of the tail code into a two-line format in white letters with the T2 prefix centered above the three-digit identifier. It also appears that No. 204 *Ku* was the only unit to surround both wing and fuselage *hinomaru* with white piping to field-painted Zeros. At least two different colours, red and yellow, were used for fuselage bands, however the unit regularly operated in three-*chutai* structures and it is possible there was a third colour. *Chutaicho* were indicated by a double fuselage band, and *shotaicho* by tail stripes.

There is some circumstantial evidence to indicate that all No. 204 *Ku*'s yellow-banded Zeros had tail code numbers below 148. The lowest red banded Zero had the aircraft number 163. Thus it can be argued that T2 169 as flown by Warrant Officer Yanagiya Kenji on the Yamamoto escort mission had a red band, although it is illustrated elsewhere as having a yellow one. Nonetheless, much in respect to No. 204 *Ku* markings including its command heraldry is unclear. More data points are required before firm conclusions and colour associations can be drawn.

Zeros T2 112 and T2 1129 are both Nakajima Model 21s seen at Buin. See notes for Profile 59 with a yellow fuselage band.

Zero T2 153 parked at Lakunai.
This airframe and the one behind
are both Model 22s.

The subject of Profile 61 is seen at
Buin in its two-tone camouflage.

T2 197 parked at Vunakanau
while a chutai of four Zeros fly
overhead.

Among the recognisable tail codes
in this line-up up Lakunai are T2
112, T2 1148 and T2 1105. Also
visible is a chutaicho Zero with
double fuselage stripes but an
unidentified tail code.

No. 204 *Kokutai*

53

T2133

54

T2157

55

T2
190

56

T2
175

Profile 53: Mitsubishi A6M3 Model 32 MN 3305, T2 133, Lieutenant (jg) Shibuya Kiyoharu 澁谷清春, ditched 23 January 1943 near Kolombangara.

This Model 32, flown by *chutaicho* Lieutenant (jg) Shibuya Kiyoharu, was ditched close to the shore of Kolombangara on 23 January 1943 after combat with VMO-251 Wildcats. This incident rates special mention as the intact wreckage was raised about a year later in May 1944, giving Allied intelligence its first opportunity to inspect the Type 99 Mk 2 20mm long-barrelled cannon. All radios and antennas were removed by the ground crew, and the tailplane had an adjustable rudder trim tab, a modification found only on the last batch of Model 32s produced. Tail code T2 133 also defines No. 204 *Ku* leadership markings during the early 1943 timeframe.

Profile 54: Mitsubishi A6M3 Model 32 MN 3202, T2 157, captured at Munda August 1943.

This Zero was previously tail code 1152 with No. 252 *Ku* (see Profile 77) and was captured at Munda airfield in August 1943. Referenced from colour photos and the resultant technical report, the previous tail code had been painted over and a new No. 204 *Ku* code applied in its place. The red fuselage band was similarly over painted, with a narrower red band applied just in front. The cowling carburettor intake had "57" painted in white.

Profile 55: Mitsubishi A6M3 Model 32 T2 190, Buka, 7 April 1943.

This Model 32 Zero was photographed at Buka on 7 April 1943 during Operation I-Go.

Profile 56: Mitsubishi A6M3 Model 22 MN 3415, T2 175, forced-landed Munda early 1943.

This A6M3 Model 22 is believed to be MN 3415 (built early January 1943), later painted in the field with a non-standard dark blue green. Sometime in the first half of 1943 it force-landed at Munda airfield, collapsing the left undercarriage, bending the propeller and structurally damaging the left wing. In August 1943 this Zero was studied by the Air Technical Intelligence Unit. It was one of only two Model 22s abandoned at Munda and was subsequently moved to Guadalcanal for further analysis. The profile is recreated from markings contained in the technical report and a colour newsreel taken on 17 September 1943 when the First Lady of the United States Eleanor Roosevelt visited Guadalcanal as part of her South Pacific tour.

Designation of this Zero by Allied intelligence as a "Zeke Mark 2" is significant. The advent of the A6M3 Type 22 in December 1942 brought about a minor change in the fuselage stencil applied by Mitsubishi, as the Navy at that time had not resolved which designation should be allocated to the A6M3 version, so it continued to use the previous designation Type Zero Mark 2 Carrier-based Fighter. How long this practice remained is uncertain, but Mitsubishi later changed the template to a three-line stencil with the adoption on 29 January 1943 of the designation for the longer-winged A6M3 Model 22 variant.

No. 204 *Kokutai*

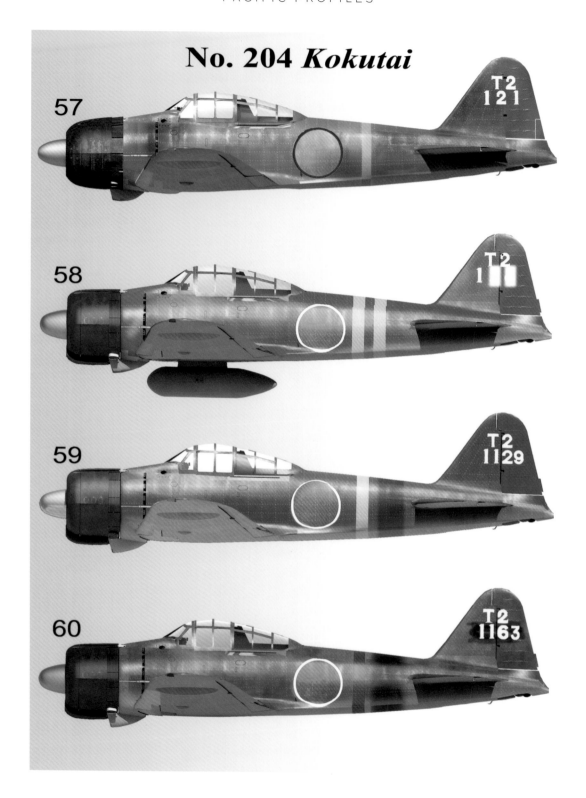

57

58

59

60

Profile 57: Mitsubishi A6M3 Model 22 T2 121, Buka, 7 April 1943.

This Model 22 Zero was painted in the field with a non-standard dark blue green similarly to T2 175, and was photographed at Buka on 7 April 1943 during Operation I-Go.

Profile 58: Nakajima A6M2, T2 1??, Lakunai late 1943,

hikotaicho Lieutenant Okajima Koji 岡島康治.

This profile (with two blocks representing unknown digits) references a photo taken at Lakunai, Rabaul, in mid-1943. The camouflage is field-applied, and the twin fuselage bands indicate a *chutaicho*, likely Lieutenant Okajima Koji who later replaced Lieutenant Commander Shindo Saburo in September 1943. It is possible that junior lieutenants performing the role of *chutaicho* had one fuselage band and twin tail stripes as in the case of T2 133, however this is unconfirmed. In most field-applied schemes, the manufacturer's stencil was painted over.

Profile 59: Nakajima A6M2 T2 1129 (previously 1129 with No. 252 *Ku*), Buin, 7 April 1943.

An enduring mystery for many years was why several No. 204 *Ku* Zeros had four digits in their tail codes instead of three. This is because at end of February 1943 several Zeros were transferred into the unit from No. 252 *Ku* which had employed a non-hyphenated code of four numerals (along with a wide red fuselage band). On this particular Zero this band was painted over and a yellow one applied, and the T2 prefix was applied over the earlier four-digit numeral. T2 1129 was thus previously 1129 with No. 252 *Ku*, and was photographed at Buin on 7 April 1943.

Profile 60: Nakajima A6M2 MN 5452, T2 1163 (previously 1122 with No. 252 *Ku*),

captured Vila airfield, Kolombangara.

The profile is created from extensive photography of the intact wreck. This aircraft was transferred to No. 204 *Ku* from No. 252 *Ku* at the end of February 1943. Originally it had the tail code 1122 and a wide red fuselage band as seen in Profile 71. The earlier tail code was painted over with a darker green and replaced with the new tail code of T2 1163. The wide red fuselage band was likewise removed and a new narrower red one applied in its place. The leading edge identification markings were unusually deep and extended backwards on the lower wing, covering the wheel well covers.

No. 204 *Kokutai*

61

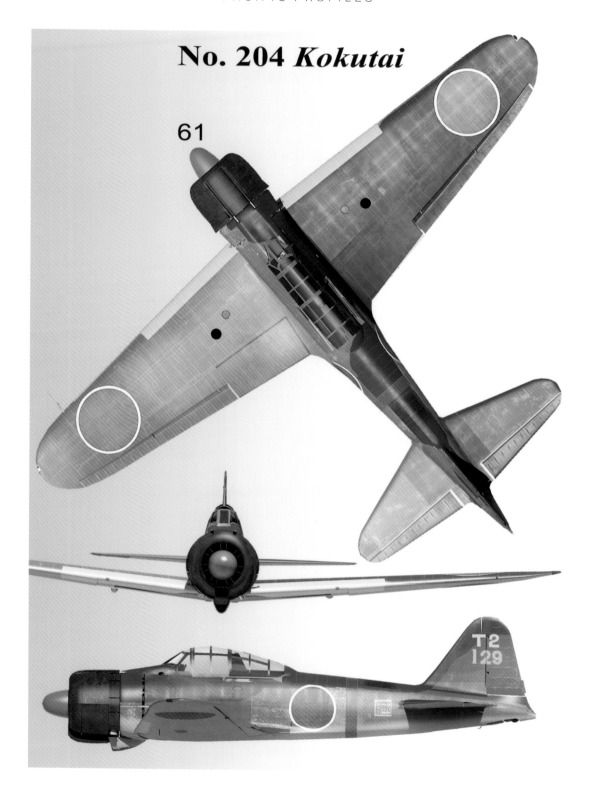

Profile 61: Nakajima A6M2 T2 129, Buin, May 1943.

This Zero, referenced from a photo taken at Buin, had an unusual field camouflage scheme, being divided almost symmetrically in two-tone green.

The wreck of this No. 204 Ku Zero was photographed on Guadalcanal in 2020. The overturned upper wing surface, protected from the elements for many years, shows one of the green shades field-applied at Rabaul.

The subject of Profile 66 departs a Bougainville airfield.

The subject of Profile 63, and perhaps the most famous Zero photo ever taken. However, it is doubtful the pilot is FCPO Nishizawa Hiroyoshi as is so often claimed. Nonetheless, the photo showcases the ad hoc nature of early No. 251 Ku markings.

CHAPTER 9
No. 251 *Kokutai*

After the Tainan *Ku* was redesignated No. 251 *Ku* in the 1 November 1942 IJN restructure, it returned to Japan the week later to regroup and retrain. Nonetheless the newly renamed unit conducted several missions in New Guinea before departing, the last being an interception of B-17s near Lae on 5 November led by the *chutaicho* Lieutenant Kawai Shiro.

Once back in Japan the unit retained Captain Kozono Yasuna as *hikocho* (thus becoming known as the "Kozono *Buntai*") and Lieutenant Commander Nakajima Tadashi as *hikotaicho*. It kept 11 pilots from the surviving Tainan *Ku* cadre as its core, and Lieutenant Mukai Ichiro was appointed *buntaicho*. No. 251 *Ku* also received new Model 22 Zeros with which to begin training at Toyohashi in early 1943. All of these aircraft were allocated the tail code prefix "U1".

With training completed, the *kokutai* was assigned back to the South Seas under the command of the 25th *Koku Sentai*. However, Lieutenant Commander Nakajima stayed behind in Japan and Lieutenant Mukai was appointed *hikotaicho* in his place. The unit sailed from Yokosuka for Truk on 25 April 1943 with its aircraft aboard the carriers *Unyo* and *Chuyo* which were escorted by four destroyers. In Truk Harbour the Model 22s were craned onto barges and then ferried ashore before being flown to Rabaul in two groups. The first delivery flight of Zeros landed at Lakunai on 10 May 1943 after an uneventful flight cruising at 150 knots. The arrival of the second detachment brought the unit's total fighter complement to 58 Zeros which were then supplemented by seven J1N2 Irving reconnaissance twins and four G4M1 Betty transports, all flown separately to Rabaul.

The No. 251 *Ku*'s first mission was a two-hour reconnaissance conducted by a J1N2 Irving from Lakunai on 13 May 1943. The next day Lieutenant Mukai Ichiro led 33 Zeros to escort Bettys in a morning attack against Oro Bay. There they encountered fierce enemy resistance, and although they lost no fighters, five Model 22s were damaged by gunfire. The unit then flew two remarkable long-distance missions on 21 and 22 May 1943, both venturing into the mountainous area over the small towns of Bulolo and Wau south-west of Lae. There they engaged P-38 Lightnings and Liberators on the first mission, claiming three P-38s and one B-24 while in fact no US aircraft were lost. The combat extended the mission duration to a lengthy six and a half hours, which No. 251 *Ku* repeated the following day, leaving Rabaul shortly after dawn. However, no enemy opposition was encountered on this second strike.

On 7 June 1943 the unit flew its first major sweep in the Solomons against the Russell Islands in company with Nos. 204 and 582 *Ku* Zeros. This involved a sizeable formation of 36 No. 251 *Ku* Zeros staged through Buka from Rabaul that morning, again led by Lieutenant Mukai Ichiro. This time aerial combat cost six Zeros and pilots. Less than a week later, on 12 June, Lieutenant O'ono Takeyoshi, of Tainan *Ku* pedigree, led 32 Zeros back to the same target, losing four Zeros and another destroyed during an emergency landing. O'ono led 30 Zeros during an attack against shipping off Lunga Point on Guadalcanal four days later. The engagement cost the No. 251 *Ku* six Zeros, including two *chutaicho*, Lieutenants O'oya Shuhei and Hoashi Takashi. This meant the unit had lost 17 Zeros to aerial combat in just three missions, a severe and unsustainable attrition rate.

On the last day of June, No. 251 *Ku* and several other Zero units sortied to oppose the American landings at Rendova on New Georgia island. This was a disastrous battle both in terms of morale and resources. Of the two dozen No. 251 *Ku* Zeros which flew the mission led by Lieutenant Mukai Ichiro, eight were shot down or went missing, two incurred serious damage with pilots badly wounded, one was destroyed back at Rabaul when it crash-landed and six more were badly damaged by gunfire. As well, the core of the unit's leadership was eradicated: *buntaicho* Mukai was shot down and Lieutenants Hashimoto Mitsuteru (No. 4 *chutai chutaicho*) and O'ono Takeyoshi (No. 2 *chutai chutaicho*) both failed to return.

Such had been the attrition rate in June 1943 that operational leadership now defaulted to a junior officer, Lieutenant (jg) Oshibuchi Takashi. But although No. 251 *Ku* was withdrawn to Rabaul, it continued operations in the Solomons until 1 September 1943 when the unit was reclassified as a night fighter unit using the converted version of the J1N2 Irving. From the time the unit first arrived in Rabaul on 10 May until the end of August 1943 it lost 34 pilots and many Zeros destroyed due to combat. Its surviving Zero inventory was subsequently dispersed among Rabaul's other fighter units, including No. 253 *Ku*.

Unit Markings

No. 251 *Ku*'s new Model 22 Zeros were camouflaged in a variety of dark green wavy schemes (including spinners) after leaving Japan, although it is not clear exactly when this was done. No two camouflage patterns were alike, and they were applied by a variety of methods including brush, cloth dipped in paint or spray gun, limited only by artistic imagination and dexterity. Due to the heavy attrition rate of airframes, within a couple of months most of the initial batch of new Model 22s had been replaced by Model 22s coming off Mitsubishi's production lines. These newer Zeros had factory-applied upper surface dark overall green camouflage.

The U1-1?? tail codes originally applied in Japan were black and not red as incorrectly depicted in illustrations elsewhere (Hata and Izawa also concur the code was black). Regardless, these black codes were over-painted when the field-applied camouflage schemes became extant, and the three-digit codes were repainted in white, with the black "U1" remaining over-painted. Most aluminium-painted spinners had camouflage applied as well, again to varying degrees. Factory green Model 22s at first had spinners painted with aluminum paint until the entire prop assembly was painted red brown towards the end of 1943.

A series of airborne photos, taken on 23 May 1943 during one of the first missions over the Solomons, show the following No. 251 *Ku* Model 22s with the prefix "U1" either painted over or barely visible and the remaining tail codes painted in white: 105, 109, 152, 162 and 163.

Other photos and documentary evidence provide codes 113, 126, 150, 157, 158, 161, 183, 184, U1-106, U1-162 and another in the U1-12? range. The same photos also show one example of a single tail stripe and angled fuselage band (unknown tail code), one of a single tail stripe and double angled fuselage bands (158) and one of a double tail stripe (163). By July 1943 the unit often operated four-aircraft *shotai* for larger missions, sometimes with 12 fighter *chutai* formations. Based on operational assignments from the unit's *kodochosho*, it appears the following chutai structure was implemented:

- No.1 *chutai* Lieutenant O'ono Takeyoshi

- No.2 *chutai* Lieutenant (jg) Koshita Takashi

- No.3 *chutai* Lieutenant (jg) Hashimoto Mitsuteru

- No.4 *chutai* Lieutenant (jg) Oshibuchi Takashi.

An additional *chutaicho* in this timeframe was Lieutenant (jg) O'oya Shuhei.

A line-up of No. 251 Ku Zeros at Lakunai in early June 1943 shows a range of unorthodox camouflage schemes. One of the unit's transport G4M1s can be seen in the background.

Zero Model 22 tail code 184 departs from Buin, although it is possible this fighter was serving with No. 253 Ku at the time.

No. 251 *Kokutai*

62

63

64

65

Profile 62: Mitsubishi A6M3 Model 22, U1-162, Toyohashi, Japan, April 1943.

This Model 22 was photographed while still in Japan during which time FCPO Nishizawa Hiroyoshi was also photographed both sitting in U1-106, and next to another Model 22 coded U1-12?. The unit removed all antennas shortly after they received the Zeros. It appears likely that the Model 22s arrived in Rabaul before the application of field-applied camouflage.

Profile 63: Mitsubishi A6M3 Model 22 105, Rabaul, 23 May 1943,
flown (allegedly) by FCPO Nishizawa Hiroyoshi 西澤広義.

A much-published series of air-to-air photos allegedly showing FCPO Nishizawa Hiroyoshi flying (U1-)105 on an early mission over the Solomons were taken on 23 May 1943. These Model 22 Zeros were among the original batch assigned in Toyohashi with the black U1 prefix over-painted. The photos were taken on behalf of photographer Yoshida Hajime, a Nichiei journalist who visited Rabaul, Lae, Buin and Ballale throughout 1942-43. No specific mention of Nishizawa is made in Yoshida's autobiography *Samurai Reisen Kisha*. As Yoshida had become friendly with Nishizawa, who by then had acquired legendary status, it seems improbable that Yoshida would not have mentioned him as being pilot of the relevant Zero. It appears Yoshida lent his camera to a pilot, possibly Nishizawa himself, since other photos from the same sequence clearly show the outer segments of a Zero wing. Regardless, there is no evidence to support the assertion that (U1-)105 was being flown by Nishizawa that day, and the origins of this contention are unclear. In addition, Zero (U1-)105 carries no *shotaicho* markings although Nishizawa flew every combat mission in that role. *Shotaicho* Zeros were not assigned to pilots in No. 251 *Ku*, rather they were allocated on each mission.

It appears that the camouflage was applied by spray gun, likely by someone who sometimes held the gun too close to the surface, resulting in several narrow and heavy passes. In their attempt to cover much of the airframe they have, perhaps inadvertently, produced an expedient mottle. It is difficult to accurately recreate the scheme as it was applied on an arbitrary basis.

Profile 64: Mitsubishi A6M3 Model 22 109, Rabaul, 23 May 1943.

It appears that (U1-)109's camouflage scheme was applied by brush and showcases a different and more economical camouflage appearance.

Profile 65: Mitsubishi A6M3 Model 22 163, Rabaul, May 1943.

There are three extant photos of "163" when it served with No. 251 *Ku*; one without tail stripes, and one with two stripes as portrayed here. A later photo of the same airframe shows the tail code as 2-163 with the same two tail stripes and two *chutaicho* fuselage stripes. Zero 2-163 was the same aircraft but part of the Rabaul Air Force (see Chapter 13) and photographed in service after No. 251 *Ku* transferred its inventory to other units.

No. 251 *Kokutai*

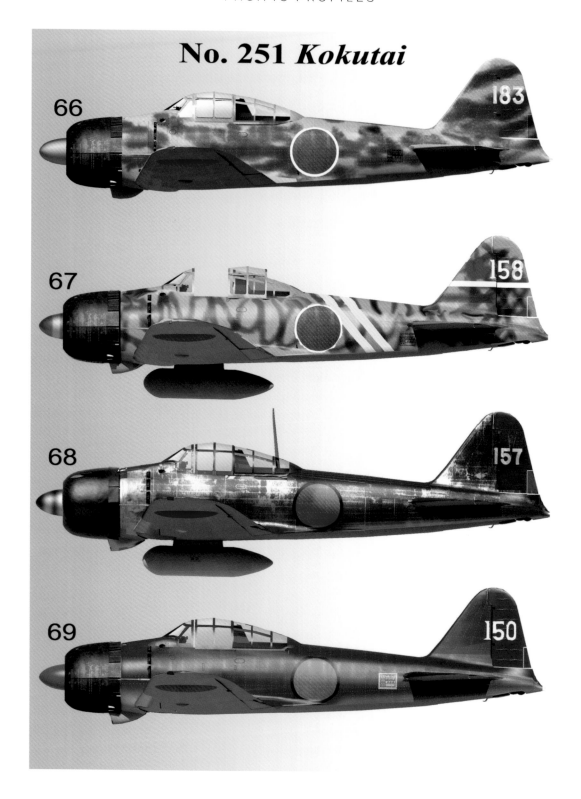

66

67

68

69

Profile 66: A6M3 Model 22 183, Buka, April 1943.

This Model 22 was photographed at Buka around May 1943. The mottled camouflage scheme was applied with a wide nozzle spray brush. It is possible that the fighter was serving with No. 253 *Ku* and not No. 251 *Ku* at the time of the photo.

Profile 67: A6M3 Model 22 158, Lakunai, May 1943.

This *chutaicho* Zero was photographed at Lakunai in mid-1943 and is one of the Model 22s originally brought from Japan. The double fuselage stripes indicate a *chutaicho* aircraft, and photos suggest it had the previous tailcode U1-158, with the "U1" painted over. The "snake-weave" camouflage has been applied sparingly with a spray gun at moderate air pressure.

Profile 68: A6M3 Model 22 157, Lakunai, August 1943.

This aircraft was photographed taking off at Lakunai in August 1943 and appears to be a replacement Model 22 with heavily weathered factory-applied camouflage.

Profile 69: Mitsubishi A6M3 Model 22 150, Buin, July 1943,

FPO1c Tsujioka Tamotsu 辻岡將 shot down 12 July 43, New Georgia.

On 12 July 1943 FPO1c Tsujioka Tamotsu was shot down and captured after parachuting into the waters of Enogai Inlet on the coast of New Georgia. He told his captors that his tail code of 150 had no prefix and his Zero was overall dark green. This fits the description of the factory-camouflaged Model 22s which had recently started appearing in the No. 251 *Ku* inventory as badly needed replacements. Note these aircraft had spinners painted green in the field.

The tail of 1148 which force-landed on the beach at Cape Esperance, Guadalcanal, on 25 January 1943. This No. 252 Ku airframe carries no chutaicho or shotaicho markings.

The white surround hinomaru on Nakajima Model 21 Zero tail code 1148, is clearly visible in this photo. The tail code was hand-painted and other less clear photos have led to an incorrect interpretation of the tail code as 1146.

CHAPTER 10
No. 252 *Kokutai*

When created from the fighter wing of the Genzan *Ku*, No. 252 *Ku* had its authorised strength increased from three dozen to 60 Zeros. The new unit was assigned to the 22nd *Koku Sentai*, and initially trained at Tateyama in Japan. Meanwhile, on 30 October 1942 five Model 21 and 21 Model 32 Zeros were loaded aboard the aircraft carrier *Taiyo* which arrived at Rabaul on 9 November. Captain Yanagimura Yoshitane was appointed *hikocho* and Lieutenant Suganami Masaji as *hikotaicho*.

No. 252 *Ku's* introduction to theatre operations was luckless when it lost two batches of Zeros in separate weather events. The fighters were flown off *Taiyo* to Lakunai and two days later their first mission, led by *chutaicho* Lieutenant Yamamoto Shigehisa, was carried out over the Solomons alongside Zeros from Nos. 253 and 582 *Ku*. Only a few days later, on 13 November, Yamamoto led six junior pilots (all except one were Superior Seamen) on a combat air patrol to defend the damaged battlecruiser *Hiei* returning to Rabaul. Heavy cloud and squalls impeded their task; nonetheless Yamamoto's flyers circled and guarded *Hiei* for one and a half hours in the early afternoon, encountering no enemy opposition. With his duty completed, for another two hours Yamamoto tried to find a way home through the murk as five inexperienced pilots clung to his Zero. Finally, at 1615 hours, he ditched in Rekata Bay followed shortly afterwards by the others, a loss of all six fighters. All the pilots were rescued and returned to Rabaul, however Yamamoto, who had badly impacted his head during the ditching, had to be repatriated to Japan for long-term medical treatment.

The bad luck continued. On the next day, 14 November, *hikotaicho* Suganami led six Model 21 Zeros on a defensive patrol to cover a destroyer run tasked to deliver the 38th Division to Guadalcanal. Whilst trying to attack a formation of eight B-17 Flying Fortresses, they were heavily engaged and scattered by a dozen VF-10 Wildcats from the carrier *Enterprise* in half an hour of intense combat. Although Suganami met with his comrades at the agreed rendezvous en route back to Rabaul, he never made it home. It appears likely he was wounded in the combat, perhaps by VF-10 pilot Lieutenant John Sutherland who claimed a "Nagoya Zero" from the encounter. Lieutenant Suho Motonari then replaced Suganami as *hikotaicho*. For its part, No. 252 *Ku* claimed 14 "Grummans" from this afternoon fight, more than were airborne. In fact, not one Wildcat was lost.

The unit detached a *chutai* to Lae and Buna on 20 November, led by Lieutenant (jg) Chikanami Isahiro. Another detachment moved to Ballale, and then, when Munda was opened to air operations on 23 December 1942, 21 No. 252 *Ku* Zeros proceeded there, accompanied by nine more from No. 204 *Ku*. However, in the following two days 11 No. 252 *Ku* Zeros were damaged or destroyed at Munda airfield by Allied bombing attacks.

This unlucky No. 252 *Ku* again lost several Zeros to bad weather on 25 January 1943 when four air groups launched 76 Zeros down The Slot to conduct a fighter sweep. Of No. 252 *Ku*'s 18 Zeros, seven were downed in a weather front. Three were ditched and one landed wheels-up on the beach near the village of Visale on Guadalcanal's northwest tip. Although these first four pilots were rescued, the other three disappeared. On 1 February 1943 the unit was ordered to transfer to the Marshall Islands however the move was delayed pending the completion of Operation Ke, the evacuation of Guadalcanal. By the time No. 252 *Ku* had moved to the Marshalls, it had undergone a brief but costly four-month South Seas deployment, losing 16 pilots to combat or weather accidents.

Unit Markings

When No. 252 *Ku* arrived in theatre, all Japanese ground-based air units in the Guadalcanal campaign were assigned to either the 21st and 26th *Koku Sentai* under the command of the South East Area Fleet and 11th Air Fleet respectively. However, No. 252 *Ku* had been detached from its parent 22nd *Koku Sentai* along with No. 582 *Ku*'s fighter wing when it moved to Rabaul. During their time in theatre both these Zero contingents were rotated between the two Rabaul-based *Koku Sentai* as required in a "roving commission".

The key to rationalising IJN air unit codes lies in the IJN Order of Battle. Without formal air flotilla assignment, the fighter wings of both Nos. 252 *Ku* and 582 *Ku* comprised the 1st Air Attack Force, an operational structure. In doing so they adopted the numerals "1" and "2" as tail code prefixes, but in a break from normal practice their tail codes were applied without hyphens. The three-digit individual plane number followed immediately without space separation, resulting in Zero tail codes for No. 252 *Ku* in the 11?? format and No. 582 *Ku* in the 21?? format. These tail codes were applied in red. Whilst this independent assignment predicated the atypical tail code system, note that No. 582 *Ku*'s D3A2 dive-bombers remained attached to the 26th *Koku Sentai* and thus retained their T3 prefix.

Fortunately, No. 252 *Ku* were forced to abandon numerous Zero airframes at Munda from which definitive markings were documented. Its signature marking was a single wide red fuselage band, but it is unknown how *chutaicho* and *shotaicho* aircraft were marked, or even if they carried any distinctive command markings. Note also that the unit's Zeros did not use the "Y2" prefix in the South Seas theatre; this was used later in the Marshall Islands when No. 252 *Ku* was reassigned back to the 22nd *Koku Sentai*. The wrecked Zeros inspected on Munda in August 1943 give clear evidence of the unit's 11?? format tail code, as so do two of the four Zeros downed near Cape Esperance on 25 January 1943.

The subject of Profile 74 as it lay in shallow water the day after it ditched at Cape Esperance, Guadalcanal.

The subject of Profile 76 on Ballale Island taken a few months after the island's capture.

The subject of Profile 70 at Lakunai, with the unit's wide red band just visible. A lack of clarity on other photos can confuse the unorthodox numeral 2 with the letter Z.

No. 252 *Kokutai*

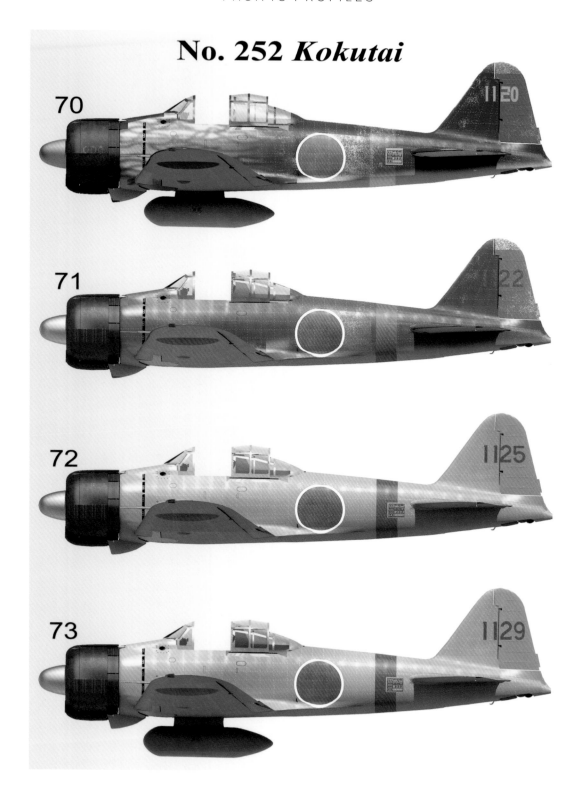

70

71

72

73

Profile 70: Nakajima A6M2 Model 21, 1120, Lakunai.

This Model 21 Zero was photographed at Lakunai with only the last two digits clearly visible. The "2" appears in some photos as a "Z", leading to past speculation as to the fighter's unit association. The camouflage scheme is abnormal too; a snake-weave on the forward fuselage leading to progressive overall green as the pattern moves rearwards. Unusually the code was painted in yellow and not red.

Profile 71: Nakajima A6M2 Model 21 MN 5452, 1122,

(subsequently T2 1163 with No. 204 *Ku*).

This Model 21 Zero was transferred to No. 204 *Ku* at end of February 1943, and was later abandoned by that unit at Vila airfield, Kolombangara (see Profile 60). Overall green paint application in the field was unusually light on No. 252 *Ku* airframes, which quickly gave way to weathering.

Profile 72: Nakajima A6M2 1125, lost 25 January 1943.

An IJN message log dated 25 January 1943 queried Munda as to the whereabouts of Zero 1125, thus providing the tail code for this Model 21. Note how the red fuselage band is cut away to make room for the Nakajima manufacturing stencil.

Profile 73: Nakajima A6M2 1129, wrecked at Munda.

This airframe was destroyed on the ground at Munda between late December 1942 and mid-March 1943.

No. 252 *Kokutai*

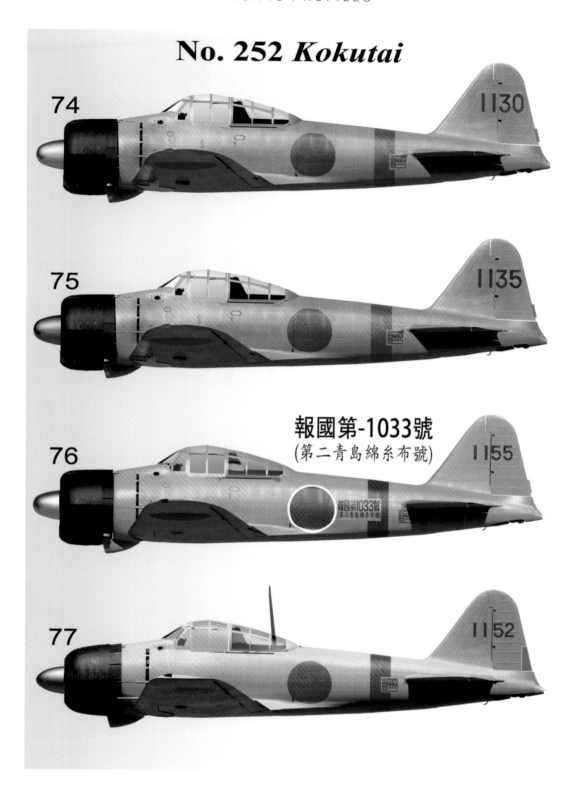

74 1130

75 1135

報國第-1033號
(第二青島綿糸布號)

76 1155

77 1152

Profile 74: Nakajima A6M2 MN 7236, 1130, ditched off Guadalcanal, 25 January 1943.

This Model 21 Zero ditched in shallow water off Guadalcanal on 25 January 1943, one of four that ditched or beached in the area.

Profile 75: Nakajima A6M2 MN 2182, 1135, abandoned at Munda.

This airframe was abandoned at Munda between late December 1942 and mid-March 1943. Note how the red fuselage band has been cut away to accommodate the Nakajima fuselage stencil.

Profile 76: Nakajima A6M2 Model 21 MN 3471, 1155, HK-1033, abandoned on Ballale.

This Nakajima Model 21 Zero was found on Ballale Island. It was photographed in November 1945 by a New Zealand photographer attached to an Australian Army detachment tasked with searching out details of POW gravesites on the island. The subscript for HK-1033 indicates the donor, as it notes the Zero was the second aircraft donated by Tsingtao Cotton Fabric. This likely was a company named Tsingtao Menshifu, or it might represent a conglomerate of textile companies located in Tsingtao, China. The MN is unknown but a tail fin with the last two digits "55" was recovered from a proximate location and it is possibly linked with HK-1033.

Profile 77: Mitsubishi A6M3 Model 32 MN 3116, 1152,

(subsequently T2 157 with No. 204 *Ku*).

This Zero was captured at Munda airfield in August 1943. The previous tail code had been over-painted, and a new No. 204 *Ku* code was applied in its place. However, with careful examination of photos of the tail it is possible to make out the last two digits of the tail code: "52". The wide fuselage band was similarly over-painted, but it fits with the fuselage band size and location used by No. 252 *Ku*. Thus it is deduced that this Model 32 Zero was originally part of No. 252 *Ku* with the tail code of 1152.

A gun camera caught Model 52 Zero tail code 53-112 over Rabaul around late 1943.

The subject of Profile 81 departs Lakunai.

CHAPTER 11
No. 253 *Kokutai*

On 1 October 1942 (one month earlier than the wider IJN restructure), the Kanoya *Ku* was renamed No. 751 *Ku*, and then on 1 November its fighter wing was detached and made into a separate fighter unit, designated No. 253 *Ku*. The new fighter unit was attached to the 21st *Koku Sentai*, retaining Commander Kobayashi Yoshito as *hikocho*. Its authorised strength was increased to 48 fighters.

At the same time No. 253 *Ku* also operated two D4Y1-C Judy reconnaissance aircraft, at least one J1N1-C reconnaissance aircraft and then in February 1943 it added four Ki-46 Dinah reconnaissance aircraft. The latter arrived at Rabaul just in time to be deployed during Operation I-Go, where they were shared operationally with No. 204 *Ku*. This reconnaissance detachment was commanded by Lieutenant Kofuru Yoshio. All the aircraft and personnel of the detachment were subsequently transferred to No. 151 *Ku* shortly after it was activated at Rabaul on 15 April 1943.

Lieutenant Ito Toshitaka, who arrived at Kavieng on 19 September 1942, was appointed *hikotaicho*, with his deputy Lieutenant Kawai Shiro. Among the first batch of pilots to arrive at Rabaul in late January 1942 with the Chitose *Ku*, Kawai had since built up a fine reputation in both No. 4 *Ku* and the Tainan *Ku*. The new *kokutai* remained first at Kavieng before moving to Rabaul, however substantial No. 253 *Ku* detachments eventually served throughout all South Seas bases, including at Gasmata, Buka, Ballale, Lakunai and Buin.

A full *chutai* of nine fighters was detached to Gasmata in February 1943 for air defence purposes. On 19 February No. 253 *Ku* lost its first officer pilot when the entire *chutai*, led by Lieutenant I'itsuka Masaya, intercepted and shot down the 90th Bombardment Group Liberator *Lady Lucy*. Two junior lieutenants, Saito Saburo and Kenmochi Yoichi, led Nos. 2 and 3 *shotai* respectively for this mission. However, during the combat Kenmochi was shot down by return fire from the Liberator's gunners.

No. 253 *Ku* also participated in attacks against Oro Bay and the closing stages of the Guadalcanal campaign. During Operation I-Go it performed fighter sweeps, airfield defence and convoy protection duties. In May 1943 the unit was withdrawn to Saipan in order to re-equip and recuperate and its authorised strength was increased to 96 Zeros. Lieutenant I'itsuka Masaya was reassigned to another unit at Saipan, and Lieutenant (jg) Saito Saburo was appointed *hikotaicho*. One *chutai*, under his command, was briefly dispatched to Buin in early July to participate in the Rendova campaign. Saito was lost over Rendova on 15 July 1943 along with two other pilots, and Lieutenant Ito Toshitaka was appointed as acting *hikotaicho*. The week after this fateful mission the detachment's pilots were again returned to Saipan, leaving behind their Zeros which were reassigned to other units in the 26th *Koku Sentai*.

On 18 August 1943 Lieutenant Commander Okamoto Harutoshi, who had been *hikotaicho* of the No. 4 *Ku* fighter wing in early 1942 and had since spent time in Japan, was posted to No.

253 *Ku*, replacing Lieutenant Ito Toshitaka who had been acting as *hikotaicho*. Then in early September 1943 the unit again returned to Rabaul (Tobera) as the only fighter unit in the 25th *Koku Sentai*. It became increasingly involved in the defence of Rabaul as fighting intensified during the October/November Fifth Air Force campaign against Rabaul, later taken up by Allied units from the Solomons. In this timeframe No. 253 *Ku* also was a major participant during Operation Ro-Go. Okamoto remained *hikotaicho* throughout this challenging time, serving with No. 253 *Ku* until 19 January 1944. Stemming from Okamoto's defence of Rabaul, a *gunka* (patriotic war song) was composed in Japan titled *Souretsu! Okamoto Butai* (Hail the Heroic Okamoto Unit) which lauded the heroic achievements of No. 253 *Ku*.

Throughout late 1943 No. 253 *Ku* continued to also involve itself in the New Guinea theatre. A particularly fierce fight took place on the morning of 17 October when 28 of the unit's fighters joined 32 Zeros from No. 204 *Ku* for a fighter sweep over Oro Bay. Here they engaged 475th FG Lightnings and 49th FG Warhawks. During the intense combat the unit lost five pilots, including Lieutenant (jg) Sagara Haruo, while No. 204 *Ku* lost three Zeros. American losses totalled three Lightnings and one Warhawk, reflecting that even at this later stage of the South Seas conflict, No. 253 *Ku* was still mounting offensive operations.

By the end of January 1944, No. 253 *Ku* was the only unit able to credibly defend Rabaul as the severe attrition rate had worn down all other fighter units, including the recently arrived Zeros of the Second Carrier Division. Then, despite overwhelming odds, on 9 February 1944 *chutaicho* Lieutenant (jg) Ito Toshio led two dozen Zeros from Tobera to intercept a sizeable incoming combined USN and Thirteenth Air Force formation. In nearly an hour of combat the Japanese pilots fought P-38s, F4Us, TBFs, B-25s and B-24s. Only one Zero was lost, that flown by Ito himself.

The unit's last major combat took place on 19 February 1944, a mission which marked the last time a formation of Zeros defended Rabaul's skies. A force of 26 Zeros, about half of which were Model 52s, fought USN fighters for nearly an hour commencing at 0920. In this combat the last Zero pilot lost to combat over Rabaul, Superior Seaman Yamaguchi Saichi, was shot down and killed, with two more No. 253 *Ku* pilots missing. At dawn on 20 February the whole unit prepared to retreat to Truk. Their 23 remaining fighters departed Tobera at 0630 for a four-and-a-half-hour ferry flight, leaving behind two Zeros requiring maintenance. These were later rendered airworthy by the 105th Base Unit.

Unit Markings

When first established, No. 253 Ku was allocated the tail code prefix "Z1". The 21st Koku Sentai to which No. 253 Ku was first assigned also included No. 751 Ku whose G4M1 Bettys were assigned the tail code prefix "Z2". The No. 253 Ku Zeros retained their Z1 prefix when these Zeros were first field camouflaged in early 1943 and also when the new model factory camouflaged models arrived. Then, as part of a IJN-wide change in tail codes, the prefix was changed to "53" on 1 September 1943, just before the unit moved back to Rabaul from Saipan and was reassigned to the 25th *Koku Sentai*. It is possible that there was an interim period in mid-1943 where the unit simply painted over the tail prefix, just leaving a three-digit identifier similar to the way that No. 251 *Ku* marked its inventory. However, this proposition remains unconfirmed.

A published photo of field-camouflaged Model 22 Zero Z1-195 was allegedly taken at Saipan. If this is the case, this strengthens the contention that No. 253 *Ku* continued to use the official unit prefix Z1 at least until it was briefly withdrawn to Saipan in May 1943. On 15 September 1943 the unit listed an inventory of 20 Model 21s and 22 Model 22s, meaning that Model 22s were assigned into the inventory before this date. When No. 253 *Ku* replaced No. 251 *Ku* in the 25th *Koku Sentai*, all of No. 251 *Ku's* serviceable Model 22s were redistributed among Nos. 201 and 253 *Ku*. It is likely the 53 prefix was added to some of these reassigned No. 251 *Ku* Zeros, expediently keeping the original No. 251 *Ku* numbers.

It is significant that captured No. 253 *Ku* pilot Nakajima Mitsunori, who ditched on 25 January 1943 during a mission against Guadalcanal, stated during interrogation that all the unit's Zeros had a three-figure number painted on their tail. He claimed that the numbers did not run consecutively and had no special significance. Both Nos. 251 and 253 *Ku* used a white oblique fuselage stripe first for command markings and possibly later as a unit identifier. However, in the final stage of their deployment in January and February 1944 all No. 253 *Ku* Zeros adopted *Rabauru Kokubutai* prefixes. However, no rationalisation for this markings policy is verified in surviving IJN documentation (see Chapter 13 pertaining to the Rabaul *Kokubuntai*).

A6M5 tail code 53-157 written off at Lakunai as seen on 2 November 1943 when photographed during a low-level Fifth Air Force strike. Note one of the unit's reconnaissance Ki-46 Dinahs parked in the nearby revetment.

No. 253 *Kokutai*

78

ZI-182

79

53-104

80

53-157

81

53-160

Profile 78: Nakajima A6M2 Model 21, Z1-182, Gasmata, March 1943.

A photograph taken of a Model 21 based at Gasmata in March 1943 shows this tail code on a Zero which still retained an uncamouflaged olive-grey paint scheme. A second photo shows a field-camouflaged Model 22 Zero with the tail code Z1-195; the high number indicates it was probably assigned after the unit strength was raised in May 1943.

Profile 79: Mitsubishi A6M3 Model 22 or early Model 52, 53-104, Warrant Officer Iwamoto Tetsuzo 岩本徹三, Rabaul late 1943.

According to Iwamoto's memoirs, this Zero was one of two regularly flown by him. It has been portrayed by some artists as adorned with numerous pink cherry blossom victory markings, citing Iwamoto's diary. However, no photos for such markings have surfaced. Non-commissioned officers like Iwamoto flew fighters on an availability basis. The No. 253 *Ku kodochosho* shows that in early 1944 Iwamoto was sharing the unit's inventory with dozens of other pilots, and the unit operations log confirms he most often flew as a *shotaicho*. Iwamoto cites the aircraft numbers 102 and 104 as the two Zeros he most often flew, stating this information came from his logbook. However, Iwamoto's memoirs are not based on diary entries, but rather on three notebooks written about a decade after the war. Iwamoto died from post-surgery complications in 1955 at a young 38 years of age. His memoirs offer credible evidence that at least some of Rabaul's Zeros in the last few months of defending Rabaul sported victory markings. Iwamoto wrote that in January 1944:

> The number of cherry blossom victory markings on my plane increased. From a distance, it looked as though the entire rear fuselage had been re-painted pink . . . the number of victory markings on my fighter soon reached 60, no less than what had been on my previous plane. But, upon inspection by the maintenance crew, it was decided to change the engine, so I had to say farewell to my 253-102 for a while, and instead fly 253-104.

The prefix 253 was never used by the unit, and Iwamoto is doubtless referring to tail codes 53-102 and 53-104. It is likely both 102 and 104 were either late Model 22s or Model 52s with factory-applied dark green camouflage. Note this profile is thus speculative without photographic reference, and it is presented with a *shotaicho* stripe.

Profile 80: Mitsubishi A6M5 (early) Model 52, 53-157, Rabaul late 1943.

All Model 52s arrived in theatre with a factory applied dark green camouflage scheme which turned into this dull dark almost brown colour with weathering.

Profile 81: Nakajima A6M2 Model 21, 53-160, Lakunai, November 1943.

This Model 21 was photographed taking off from Lakunai in November 1943.

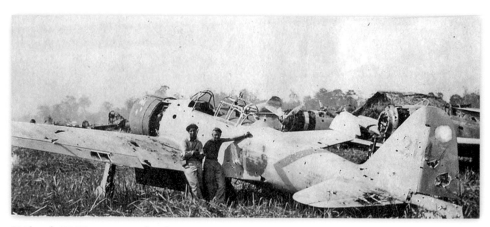

Tail code 2147 as captured at Lae.

Tail code 152 as captured at Lae and as illustrated in Profile 83.

A line-up of a mixture of Model 21 and Model 22 Zeros at Buin in April 1943 during Operation I-Go.

CHAPTER 12
No. 582 *Kokutai*

Although No. 2 *Ku* was renamed No. 582 *Ku* during the 1 November 1942 organisational restructure of the IJN, the unit's cadre continued to refer to itself as the "No. 2 *Butai*" or the "Yamamoto *Butai*" throughout its nine-month history. It remained a mixed fighter and dive-bomber unit. Commander Yamamoto Sakae remained as *hikocho* and recently promoted Lieutenant Commander Shindo Saburo was appointed *hikotaicho*. Lieutenant Kurakane Yoshio and Lieutenant Sakai Tomoyasu were the next two *chutaicho* in terms of respective seniority.

On the day of its formation on 1 November 1942 the new unit, at least in administrative terms, proceeded on its first mission: a convoy protection patrol over Guadalcanal conducted by 15 Zeros led by Lieutenant Kurakane. This was a marathon seven-and-a-half-hour early morning flight from Rabaul during which Kurakane's flyers scrapped with attacking Wildcats. Although no Zeros were damaged or lost, two had to refuel at Buka on the return journey. For the next several weeks the unit's fighters continued with similar protection missions over Guadalcanal alongside Rabaul's other fighter units.

Then, on 30 November a dozen Zeros led by Lieutenant Sakai Tomoyasu escorted six of the unit's Val dive bombers to attack Buna. The Vals refuelled en route at Gasmata and when they arrived over the target that afternoon they were challenged by 49th FG Warhawks. A fierce fight ensued from which the Zeros claimed 16 victories, but in fact no American fighters were shot down. The fight cost the Japanese two Zeros, including Sakai who was listed as missing, and a shot-up Val which was destroyed after a crash landing. The formation diverted to Lae to refuel on the way home.

Towards the end of January 1943 No. 582 *Ku* advanced to Munda and Buin to protect the destroyers evacuating Japanese troops from Guadalcanal during Operation Ke-Go. Then in April, both the unit's fighter and dive-bomber wings participated in Operation I-Go. On the morning of 18 April 1943, a few hours before Admiral Yamamoto was shot down, 16 No. 582 *Ku* Zeros led by Warrant Officer Tsunoda Kazuo scrambled from Buin at 0720 in response to an alert of an incoming formation of eight P-38s. However, they found none and landed an hour later just before Yamamoto was shot down.

Fighter sweeps and the defence of Bougainville air bases continued throughout May and June of 1943 with Lieutenant (jg) Noguchi Gi'ichi and Lieutenant (jg) Suzuki Usaburo leading many of the missions, along with Warrant Officer Tsunoda Kazuo, the most senior and experienced non-commissioned officer. At this juncture the fighter wing was still able to field three full *chutai* and large missions were sometimes led by *hikotaicho* Shindo.

The relentless pace of combat cost the life of Lieutenant (jg) Noguchi Gi'ichi on 12 June to American fighters over the Russell Islands. A more decisive mission unfolded only four days later on 16 June. Alongside Zeros from Nos. 204 and 251 *Ku*, on this fateful day 16 Zeros led by Lieutenant Commander Shindo Saburo were tasked to protect two dozen No. 582 *Ku* Vals attacking Guadalcanal. Allied fighters shot down 13 of the Vals and Shindo lost four of his Zeros.

The unit's last combat mission was flown from Buin on 12 July 1943 during which Lieutenant (jg) Suzuki Usaburo led a dozen Zeros alongside Nos. 204 and 251 *Ku* to escort a *chutai* of nine No. 582 *Ku* Vals on an uneventful bombing attack. The unit's fighter wing had by then almost fought itself to a standstill although an order to disband it was not enacted until 1 August 1943. Lieutenant Commander Shindo Saburo was then transferred to No. 204 *Ku* as its new *hikotaicho*, and most of No. 582 *Ku*'s Zero pilots were reassigned among Rabaul's other fighter units, with only a handful returned to Japan.

Unit Markings

When formed from No. 2 *Ku*, No. 582 *Ku* already comprised separate fighter and dive-bomber contingents. At this time, however, its fighter wing was detached from the parent 22nd *Koku Sentai*. For the rest of its time in theatre it, along with No. 252 *Ku*, was rotated between Rabaul's two *Koku Sentai* (the 21st and 26th) as required in a "roving commission". Both Zero units comprised the 1st Air Attack Force, and in doing so they adopted the numerals "1" and "2" as tail code prefixes, but atypically the prefixes in both cases were applied without hyphens. The three-digit individual plane number (the "1" following the initial "2" was a mission indicator - "1" for fighter) followed immediately without space separation, producing a numeric 21?? format. Despite this atypical tail code system, note that No. 582 *Ku*'s dive-bombers remained attached to the 26th *Koku Sentai* and continued to use the prefix T3.

The formation of No. 582 *Ku* required that the new tail codes be applied to the extant No. 2 *Ku* Zero inventory. This included some of the original batch Model 32s which had survived destruction at Buna. One example was *chutaicho* Zero Q-101 which became tail code 2181. Around September 1942, No. 2 *Ku* had adopted the single red chevron as its unit marking, and this chevron was retained making No. 2 *Ku* and No. 582 *Ku* the only units in theatre to use this distinctive marking.

The unit dropped the 21?? tail coding when they began applying camouflage to their aircraft around late February 1943. By late March 1943, just before the start of Operation I-Go, all the No. 582 *Ku* Zeros were so painted, along with the system of a simplified three-digit tail code. These tail codes were hand-painted in red with either white piping or "shadowing" applied to make the numerals stand out from the dark green background. At the same time the chevron marking was changed to yellow to make it more distinctive. Also around this time the unit started receiving Model 21s and 22s to supplement the Model 32s.

Some profiles incorrectly illustrate the No. 582 *Ku* chevron in this timeframe as white, but Crashed Enemy Aircraft Report #12 of 10 December 1943, (a report on a crashed No. 582 *Ku* Model 22 Val on Baanga Island near New Georgia) confirms that tail number T3-226 had a yellow chevron. Around late March 1943, when the simplified three-digit tail code was introduced, *shotaicho* markings were indicated by a shortened white stripe painted under the tail code numerals, as exemplified in Profile 87.

The unit was also the only one in the South Seas to indicate *shotaicho* fighters by cowl markings, in the case of No. 582 *Ku* a white stripe mid-cowl which extended the full length of the cowl.

Lieutenant-Commander Shindo Saburo in a new Model 22 at Buin on 16 June 1943, as illustrated in Profile 88. Note the aluminum-painted spinner and masked-off manufacturing stencil indicating this airframe was camouflaged in the factory.

The wreck of 2187 as hauled ashore Banika Island in the Russells a few days after it was shot down, the subject of Profile 85.

No. 582 *Kokutai*

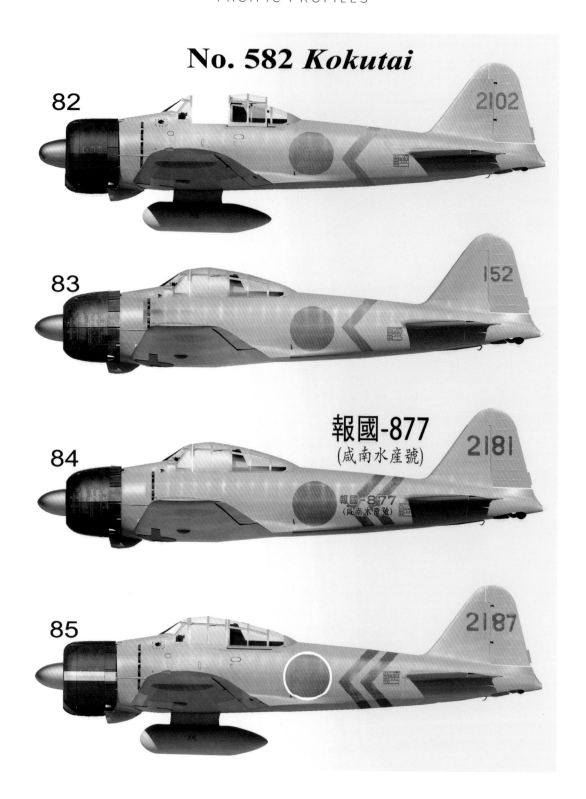

82   2102

83   152

報國-877
(咸南水産號)

84   2181

85   2187

Profile 82: Nakajima A6M2 Model 21 MN 1501, 2102 (last numeral unconfirmed), ditched Russell Islands 29 January 1943, FPO2c Horita Saburo 堀田三郎.

Pilot FPO2c Horita Saburo was shot down in the Solomons on 29 January 1943 while flying this Model 21. He provided the details of the markings of his fighter during interrogation, noting the fighters in his *chutai* were marked in the 210? range, thus the last numeral "2" in this profile is speculative. Horita also noted that many of the fighters did not have the numeral "2" prefix, demonstrating that dropping the unit prefix had started as early as January 1942, or perhaps earlier as per Profile 83.

Profile 83: Mitsubishi A6M3 Model 32 MN 3268, 152, captured Lae September 1943.

This is an early example of the new series of tail codes applied without the "2" identifying prefix. The profile is based on photos and technical reports of the aircraft found derelict at Lae.

Profile 84: Mitsubishi A6M3 Model 32 MN 3035, 2181, HK-877, Lieutenant Kurakane Yoshio 倉兼義男, abandoned at Lae.

This Model 32 Zero was previously Q-101 with No. 2 *Ku* and flown mostly by Lieutenant Kurakane Yoshio. It was damaged at Lae on an unknown date where it was abandoned and later inspected by Allied intelligence.

Profile 85: Nakajima A6M2 MN 1503, 2187, FCPO Kashimura Kanichi 樫村寛, ditched Russell Islands 6 March 1943.

This Model 21 Zero ditched off the Russell Islands following combat on 6 March 1943, killing FCPO Kashimura Kanichi. This was a fierce fight for the 18 Zeros led by Lieutenant (jg) Noguchi Gi'ichi, assigned to protect a dozen No. 582 *Ku* Vals. Both formations departed Buin at midday and the Zeros flew two minutes ahead of the Vals. They were intercepted by four Wildcats while the Vals were bombing the torpedo boat base on Banika Island. Two Vals and Kashimura's Zero were shot down, and ten additional aircraft sustained damage. The white band on the cowl is a *shotaicho* marking. Kashimura was flying as the No. 2 *shotaicho* in Noguchi's *chutai* on the day. The tail code numbers are confirmed by the engine cowling which had the last two digits "87" painted on the lower air intake. This aircraft has been illustrated incorrectly in other publications as having the tail code 2185.

No. 582 *Kokutai*

86

87

88

89

Profile 86: Mitsubishi A6M2 Model 21 191, *chutaicho* Lieutenant Suzuki Usaburo 鈴木宇三郎, Operation I-Go, April 1943.

A series of photos taken on 7 April 1943 during Operation I-Go show No. 582 *Ku* Zeros on Ballale Island, preparing to escort Vals on the strike against Guadalcanal shipping. Among them is Suzuki's Zero 191. Note the double chevron *chutaicho* marking.

Profile 87: Nakajima A6M2 Model 21 180, *shotaicho*, Operation I-Go, April 1943.

Photographed at Ballale during Operation I-Go, the short white stripe underneath the tail code indicates a *shotaicho* aircraft.

Profile 88: Mitsubishi A6M3 Model 22 173, *chutaicho* Lieutenant-Commander Shindo Saburo, Operation I-Go, April 1943.

Also photographed at Ballale on 7 April 1943 during Operation I-Go, Japanese sources state this Model 22 was flown on the mission by Shindo. The fuselage carries double yellow *chutaicho* markings.

Profile 89: Mitsubishi A6M3 Model 22 188, Operation I-Go, April 1943.

Both 188 and 185 were also photographed at Ballale on 7 April 1943 during Operation I-Go. Both tail codes had white piping instead of a white shadowing effect as seen in Profiles 86 and 88.

The subject of Profile 84, this Zero was captured at Lae in late September 1943.

Early Model 52 Zero MN 3950 and a Model 22 patrol somewhere between Rabaul and Bougainville in the later part of 1943. The A6M3 in the background is the subject of Profile 95.

A6M5 Zero 9-112 about to shut down at Lakunai in January 1944. Note the glossy reflection on the airframe from the factory finish indicating a relatively new aircraft.

CHAPTER 13
Rabaul Air Force

The *Rabauru Kokubuntai* (Rabaul Air Force) is a colloquial phrase and not an official term. Nonetheless the Zeros which saw out the last days of the fighter defence at Rabaul were commonly referred to by this name in the Japanese media at the time. They also faced the brunt of Solomons air power including the most modern Allied fighters such as F4U Corsairs and F6F Hellcats. The *Rabauru Kokubuntai* came to be regarded as a collective force by the IJN, but in reality operated and remained under extant administrative and command structures. Nonetheless, individual *kokutai* tail codes were replaced by a series of codes whose function is still unclear. The *Rabauru Kokubuntai* is described separately solely for the purposes of showcasing the many and varied markings which appeared during its operations.

As early as late June 1943 several South Seas' Zero units replaced their established unit tail codes with a tail code prefix system numbered from 1 to 9. But despite the best attempts of many historians to analyse these prefixes, they cannot definitively be correlated with specific *kokutai*. Presently, however, there are two likely but different explanations for why this system was implemented.

One possibility is that the prefixes reflected the re-organisation of the Zero inventory in the Solomons into individual maintenance groups which did not necessarily reflect their parent *kokutai*. Thus the revised codes might have been primarily used by ground crews for maintenance identification purposes. These codes would also have simplified airborne recognition.

The second possibility focuses on consolidating Rabaul's fighter command structure. In June 1943 the 26th *Koku Sentai* fighter complement was initially comprised of Zeros from Nos. 204 and 582 *Ku*. Then in early July the fighter elements from the carriers *Junyo* and *Ryuho* combined with one No. 253 *Ku chutai* to become the Bougainville-based component of the 26th *Koku Sentai*. At about the same time, on 12 July 1943 the No. 582 *Ku* Zero inventory was transferred into No. 204 *Ku*. It is thus possible that this disparate collection of fighter elements under the control of the 26th *Koku Sentai* precipitated the use of a new tail code system. From photographs it can be substantiated that this new system included the tail code prefixes of 1, 2, 4 and 6. The prefixes of 3 and 5 might have been in use at this time also, but evidence is sparse. Photographic evidence from late 1943 through early 1944 show that the prefixes of 7 and 9 were predominant. The prefix 8, although found on one A6M5 discovered on Bougainville, is too sparsely documented to draw any further conclusions about its usage.

Until the last Zero units left Rabaul in February 1944 all the unit operations logs (*kodochosho*) show that Rabaul's units often fought both in combined *kokutai* structures, as well as separately as they had always done. Thus even though these prefixes represent up to a nine *buntai* structure for the so-called Rabaul Air Force it did not necessarily change the way the units operated. Whilst there are plenty of photos from this era to provide references for accurate profiles, often these cannot be accurately dated. It is also possible that the numerical prefixes changed depending on the location and the time.

Unit Markings

The A6M5 Model 52 started to arrive in Rabaul sometime in September 1943 and were placed in service alongside Model 21s, 32s and 22s. The roster of No. 253 *Ku* lists seven Model 52s on strength as early as 1 October 43. All Model 52s left the factory painted in the same dark green upper surface camouflage which appeared in late March 1943 on mid-production Model 22s. This colour scheme, and the Southeast Area order in late August 1943 to paint over the white edges of the *hinomaru* markings, explains the "black Zero" phenomenon which appears regularly in Allied combat reports of Zeros engaged over Rabaul from late October 1943 onwards. It should also be noted that very early Model 52s retained the exhaust and cowling of the A6M3, making it often difficult at times to discern between Model 22s and Model 52s.

Aside from photographs, relevant markings of *Rabauru Kokubuntai* Zeros are also showcased in a 16mm newsreel compiled in several different timeframes, but primarily shot on 17 January 1944 by cameraman Yoshida Hajime, then assigned to the Nichiei film company. The film includes Zeros, allegedly from No. 204 *Ku* commanded by Lieutenant Yamaguchi Sadao taking off from Lakunai to intercept Allied aircraft. This newsreel shows *Rabauru Kokubuntai* tail codes on a range of Model 21, 22 and 52 Zeros with the codes 9-108, 9-112, 9-120, 9-123, 9-138, 9-155, 9-159, 9-164, 9-166, and 9-169

Furthermore, in this timeframe No. 204 *Ku* was based at Lakunai whilst No. 253 *Ku* and 2nd Carrier Division Zeros were based at Tobera. It could be argued that No. 253 *Ku* was still using the "53" tail prefix, however if this is the case the question arises as to whether all Rabaul-based Zeros in early 1944 used *Rabauru Kokubutai* coding or was it limited to just Zeros in the 26th *Koku Sentai*? Furthermore, it is unclear how the operational status of the 2nd Carrier Division was administered in this timeframe, let alone which particular markings it might have used.

The demarcation camouflage line on a factory-camouflaged late Model 21 whose tail number ends in 119, as indicated by the "19" on the undercarriage strut.

This collection of late model airframes in Japan immediately post-war shows the dark green colour applied to all IJN airframes late in the war, which became brown with exposure to the elements. This explains the many reports of "black Zeros" which appear in Allied combat reports from late 1943 onwards.

Unidentified ground crewman with A6M3 Model 22 Zero 6-171 at Lakunai in the later half of 1943. This aircraft is the subject of Profile 98.

Rabaul Air Force

90

91

92

93

Profile 90: A6M3 Model 22 1-114, Lakunai, (previously a *chutaicho* aircraft).

This Model 22 was photographed at Lakunai with several identified groundcrew from No. 201 *Ku* in the foreground. The rear fuselage has two sets of markings painted over. The single vertical band appears to indicate previous a No. 201 *Ku* assignment. Following the adoption of *Rabauru Kokubuntai* tail codes the usage of horizontal fuselage band markings seems to have been discarded. The over-painted twin oblique stripes show a likely previous *chutaicho* assignment. The demotion of this Model 22 back to common inventory reflects preference among more senior pilots for the new Model 52s with its more powerful performance. The timeframe of this profile could be October/November 1943 after the withdrawal from Buin and shortly after the advent of the newer A6M5.

Profile 91: Mitsubishi A6M3 Model 32 MN 3274, 1-151, abandoned at Buin.

The remains of this Model 32 were salvaged from Buin post-war. A caution to this profile is that it might instead be a No. 252 *Ku* Zero tail code 1151, the same numerals without the hyphen.

Profile 92: Mitsubishi A6M3 Model 22 2-116.

Believed to have been photographed at Lakunai in August 1943, this Model 22 sported a two-tone mottled green camouflage.

Profile 93: Mitsubishi A6M3 Model 22 2-163,

(previously U1-163 with No. 251 *Ku*), Buin, September 1943.

This Model 22 first served as U1-163 with No. 251 *Ku*. The twin oblique stripes on the fuselage and the two tail stripes denote a senior *chutaicho* or possibly a *hikotaicho*. This Zero has been associated by some Japanese sources with Lieutenant Kawai Shiro of No. 253 *Ku*, however the basis for this assertion is unknown.

Rabaul Air Force

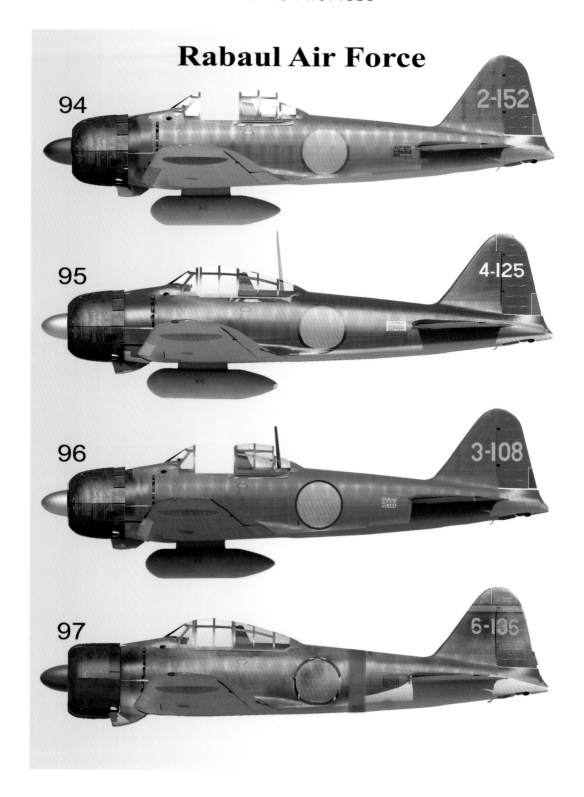

94   2-152

95   4-125

96   3-108

97   6-135

Profile 94: Mitsubishi A6M3 Model 22 MN 3844, 2-152, Bougainville 1945.

This late Model 22 was left unserviceable at Kara airfield on Bougainville in late 1943. As a morale-boosting exercise for the maintenance contingent left behind at the airfield, this Zero was made airworthy using spares from other abandoned Zeros. The project was completed by July 1945 and Rabaul was duly notified. FCPO Shibayama Sekizen was delivered by an E13A Jake from Rabaul with orders to return the Zero to Rabaul, however the war ended before he could do this.

Following the surrender of Japanese forces on Bougainville on 1 September 1945, crew from an RAAF Auster landed at Kara where they inspected the airframe. Two weeks later, after being instructed on how to fly the Zero, RNZAF Wing Commander William Kofoed flew it to Torokina with the undercarriage locked down as a safety precaution. The airframe now rests in the Auckland War Memorial Museum in New Zealand.

Profile 95: Mitsubishi A6M3 Model 22 4-125.

This Zero was photographed either near Rabaul or over Bougainville in late 1943.

Profile 96: Mitsubishi A6M5 early Model 52 MN 4043, 3-108, Rabaul 1945.

This Model 52 left the Mitsubishi factory in September 1943 in the standard dark green factory camouflage finish. At Rabaul it was assigned the tail code 3-108, and it ended the war serving with the 105th Base Unit. First surrendered at Rabaul it was subsequently flown to Jacquinot Bay on New Britain by FPO2c Shimbo Yasushi, escorted by RNZAF F4U Corsairs on 18 September 1945 alongside two other captured Zeros. The aircraft was abandoned there until salvaged in the late 1970s. The aircraft retained the cowling and exhaust of a late Model 22.

Profile 97: Nakajima A6M2 Model 21 6-136 (previously W1-187), *shotaicho*, abandoned at Buin in late 1943.

Post-war inspection of the tail code of this Model 21 revealed 6-136 painted over the previous No. 201 *Ku* code W1-187, as portrayed in Profile 52. The first tail code was painted over by brush with a darker shade of green paint and a new tail code of 6-136 was sprayed on with yellow paint and the use of a stencil. The horizontal yellow *shotaicho* stripe was spray painted on the tail above the tail code. As this was not later painted over it can be assumed the stripe remained in use with the second tail code marking.

Rabaul Air Force

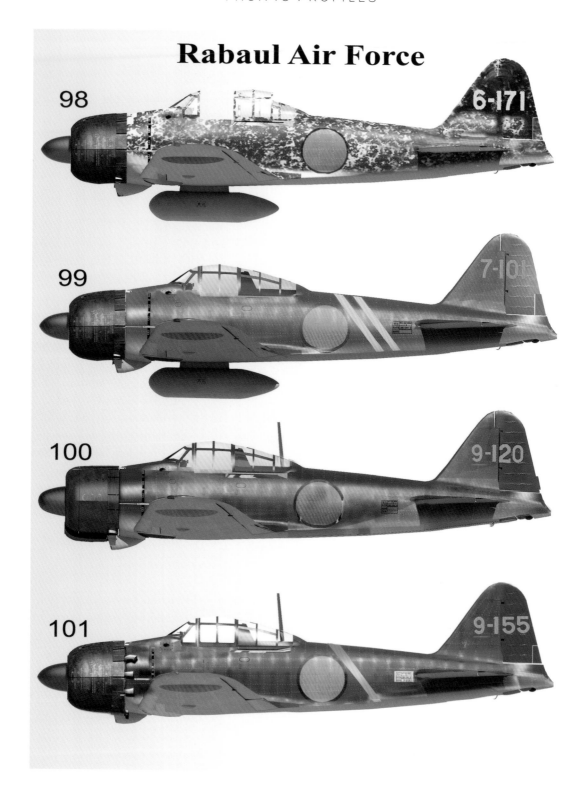

98

99

100

101

Profile 98: Mitsubishi A6M3 Model 22 6-171, Rabaul mid-1943.

Photographed at Rabaul in mid-1943, the field-applied camouflage appears to have been applied by brush. Note that before the application of the camouflage this Zero had white surrounds to the upper wing and fuselage *hinomaru,* the white edges of which were painted over with green paint, as was also the fuselage identification stencil.

Profile 99: Mitsubishi A6M3 Model 22 7-101, Rabaul, January 1944, *chutaicho* Lieutenant Yamaguchi Sadao 山口定夫.

This profile is based on a photo taken at Lakunai in late 1943 or early 1944. The double stripes on the fuselage indicates a *hikotaicho* and it is assessed it was flown often by No. 204 *Ku* division officer Lieutenant Yamaguchi Sadao who joined the unit in October 1943. Also note that this Model 22 had its lower undercarriage doors removed.

Profile 100: Nakajima A6M2 Model 21 9-120, Lakunai, January 1944.

Filmed in the aforementioned January 1943 newsreel, this A6M2 reflects several characteristics of the later production Model 21. It has both a red-brown propeller assembly and the shorter antenna of the Type 3 Model 1 radio. Also note that the lower landing gear covers have been removed.

Profile 101: Mitsubishi A6M5 Model 52 9-155, Lakunai, January 1944.

Referenced from the same film clip cited in Profile 100, this Model 52 has a single oblique fuselage *shotaicho* stripe.

A Model 52 Zero lands at Lakunai with Tavurvur volcano in the background.

Sources – General

This study draws exclusively from primary sources. Many previously published profiles have been copied or repeated in other publications, compounding and repeating numerous mistakes, including wrong *hokoku* subscripts. Zero markings are a giant jigsaw, but clues are everywhere; even Vice Admiral Kusaka Jinichi's diary contains clues on command structures which translate into wider understanding of markings systems. A highlight in this work is an update on the markings of the Tainan *Kokutai*. These have been slightly revised since those published in *Eagles of the Southern Sky* – the history of the Tainan *Ku* in New Guinea - thanks to more data points, photos and manufacturer's data plates which have come to hand since the title was published in 2013.

Two particular researchers have made seminal contributions: Ed Dekiep and Ryan Toews. Ed's close examination of the markings of the earlier units of Nos. 2, 3,4 and 6 *Ku* has been first-class. It was a pleasure collaborating with him on this arcane subject and understanding the methodical way in which he dissects matters. Similarly, but from a slightly different angle, the expertise of Ryan Toews falls into its own category of excellence. His insights on both technicalities and markings reflect a lifetime of study. His fastidious comments ensured manufacturing stencils (and their appearance or otherwise) are correctly represented in the profiles, and later model adjustable trim tabs are in situ when required. The combined firepower of Ed and Ryan has proved a force-multiplier which boosted the research quality of this work to levels I could never have achieved myself.

The author's private archival collection contains much miscellaneous information obtained over many years, which is unpractical to list. Special acknowledgement is extended for help over the years to Pacific War Air Historical Associates members Osamu Tagaya and Jim Lansdale (deceased). Special recognition to Russell Harada in Rabaul for translating more challenging handwritten *kanji*. Thanks also goes also to Ezaki Yumi in Canberra for other translation work. Nakajima manufacturer's numbers were provided by Ryan Toews per *Kogure Genkichi*.

Numerous Air Technical Intelligence Unit (ATIU) documents, IJN radio intercepts, captured diaries, Crashed Enemy Aircraft Reports (CEARs), and POW interrogations also made unique contributions. They often constitute the only primary sources which survive on several key markings.

Books & Official Publications

Senshi Sosho Vol. 96 *Nanto Homen Kaigun Sakusen*

Gatto Tesshu Go, Southeastern Area Naval Operations

Letourneau, Roger & Dennis, Operation Ke; Cactus Air Force & the Japanese Withdrawal from Guadalcanal, 2012.

Hata, Ikuhiko; Yasuho Izawa, Japanese Naval Aces and Fighter Units in World War II, 1989.

Otaka Nakajima, The Pacific War as Viewed from Combined Fleet Operations Room

Imperial Navy Magazine 29 April 1943 edition, article by reporter Takeda Michitaro

Imperial Navy Magazines 1942-45, photos numerous therein

Interrogation reports

No. 582 *Ku* pilot FPO2c Nakagawa Matao, No. 204 *Ku* pilot Leading Aircraftsman Kato Masao, *Junyo* pilots *shotaicho* Lieutenant Itesono Shiro and FCPO Kobayashi Matsutaro, (using alias Aikawa Saburo and Otani Makato during interrogations). No. 4 *Ku* pilot Nagatomo Katsuro, Tainan *Ku* pilot Kakimoto Enji, pilot Fujiden Yasuo, pilot Nakashima Mitsunori, No. 204 *Ku* pilot Sato Sumio, No. 251 *Ku* pilot Tsujioka Tamotsu and *Rabauru Kokubuntai* pilot Lieutenant (jg) Okitsu Hei'iji.

Memoirs and Diaries

Memoirs of Iwamoto Tetsuzo published 1972 by *Konnichi-no-Wadai Sha.*

Diary of No. 6 *Ku* pilot FPO1c Murakami Keijizo

Memoirs of No. 2 *Ku* Zero pilot Warrant Officer Tsunoda Kazuo

Memoirs of Commander Okumiya, staff officer to Rear Admiral Kakuta Kakuji

Diary of Vice Admiral Ugaki Matome, Chief of Staff of the Combined Fleet

Diary of Vice Admiral Kusaka Jinichi, Commander Southeast Area Fleet

Diary of Rear Admiral Sanwa Yoshiwa, Chief of Staff (aviation), Southeast Area Fleet

No. 204 *Ku* History (unofficial post-war history compiled by the veterans)

Kodochosho

Fighter units Chitose *Ku*, 2 *Ku*, 4 *Ku*, 6 *Ku*, Kanoya *Ku*, Tainan *Ku*, 201 *Ku*, 204 *Ku*, 251 *Ku*, 252 *Ku*, 253 *Ku*, and 582 *Ku*.

Logs for relevant units comprising R-Area Air Force

Allied Intelligence & Summary Reports

Documents include, *inter alia,*

CEAR #17 pertaining to Nakajima Model 21s on Kolombangara Island MNs 5359 & 5452

Army-Navy Crash Intelligence, South Pacific Area (ANCISPA) Report on Hamp 3305

ATIU Memos; numerous including No. 2, SU 1801.
Firing Equipment of the Type Zero (Mark 1, Mark 2) Provisional Handling Manual, August 1943.
ANCISPA Report, Gakken 33, p171, ATIU Memorandum No. 2,

SWPA Technical References to Inspected Enemy Airplanes, 27 September 1943.

Technical plates and markings report AWM 54 208/2/4

Appendix 'C' to Memorandum 18 pertaining to Zero manufacturing plates.

Combined Fleet Secret Op Order #19 of 1 Dec 42.

Headquarters AAF Intelligence Report, Japanese Aircraft Tail Markings, 1945.

Southeast Naval Operations part 2 (translated by US General Headquarters Far East Command, Military Intelligence Section 1952)

Numerous USN, US Marine and CACTUS Air Force Unit combat reports.

Numerous Action reports from USN, USMC and USAAF units in the Solomons 1943-44 (used as a guide only, as the aerial sightings of Japanese markings in these are mostly unreliable due to the duress of combat).

Index of Names